Recovi
Chris

Surviving Alcoholism

by

Chaplain Farris and Ruth Robertson

Published by

Recovery Literature
217 West Bennett Street
Springfield, Missouri 65807
(417) 208-5990
www.RecoveryLiterature.com
Sign up for our free encouragement newsletters.

ISBN-13: 978-0911939026
ISBN-10: 0911939024
Library of Congress Control Number: 2013902037

The self help contents of this publicaiton are solely the opinion of the author and should not be considered as a professional form of therapy, advice, treatment, direction and/or diagnosis of any kind: medical, spiritual, mental or other, nor a substitute for personalized expert advice or the services of a competent professional. The author and the Publisher assume no responsibility or liability and specifically disclaim any warranty, express or implied, for any products or services mentioned, or any techniques or practices described or utilized by the reader.

Printed in the United States of America

CONTENTS

A Personal Note from Farris and Ruth   5

Welcome to Recovery   9

The Family Photo   13

The Cycle of Addiction   19

The Alcoholic Family   29

How Far Have We Fallen   37

The Need to Feel Connected   45

How to Reconnect   51

Recovery Models   61

What Causes Alcoholism?   70

Evil is Real   77

Spiritual Encouragement   87

Faith and Works   97

Alcoholic Interventions   109

Relapse Prevention and Response   119

Spiritual Tools for Your Toolkit   133

Reminders   151

Your Next Steps   155

Index   157

A Personal Note from Farris and Ruth

We have worked with heartbreaking family situations throughout our twenty-plus year marriage and desire to bring hope to families that have become hopeless. We will be discussing alcoholism as an addiction, but there are many other addictions and you can replace the word alcohol with drugs. Indeed, substance abuse could be construed into a number of human weaknesses.

While substance use disorders include drugs, alcohol and pharmaceutical products, we will see that the addiction cycle is the same. The main difference is in the illegality of street drugs and the underworld lifestyles and subsequent legal dilemmas that accompany drug usage. Family members are often unaware that their loved one may be using a variety of substances. So, our discussions will focus on addictions in general using alcohol as the primary example. We will discuss issues related specifically to drug addictions in context as needed along the way. Remember, if a person is addicted to alcohol, they have an addiction.

None of us can "fix" a family that has been paralyzed by addiction, but God can and does. This will be the crux of our message and the reader must be ready to accept a spiritual approach with authentic willingness, open mindedness and honesty. Putting everything on the table, we will address both alcoholics and loved ones alike.

Our goals are to help you and your family discover what will turn your hopelessness to hope, to see fears driven out, and to provide your family a path to love and acceptance where there has been anger, shame, guilt, and condemnation.

If you are ready for this journey, you have already realized there is no glory in addiction and no romance in broken expectations. For your situation there seems to be no solution or hope in the world.

So, we have a greater hope to share—our hope is that you will find the unworldly answers you need, that the storm will serve to bring you to new spiritual awareness, and that you will find your life placed firmly upon the path of peace

The path of peace is not always calm, but leads to a serenity that is not easily shaken. Keep in mind that you will have to sacrifice to walk this path. You will have to be willing to be wrong. You will have to be willing to change. You will have to be willing to have grown-up adult conversations with yourself and others.

You will be tempted to make excuses and blame others and insist that they change, but they may not be able to change just because you are ready to change. Ultimately, your happiness cannot rely upon their cooperation or compliance. You have to be willing to take care of yourself first and allow others to fail if they must. Then you must also be willing to find a way for that failure to exist without it creating an environment of failure.

You might feel there are circumstances that seem impossible and complications that make no change or victory possible. We have good news for you—your feelings of despair are only feelings, not facts. Despair will slowly and surely leave the home as each family member grows, starting with you. We have seen impossible situations transformed this way many times.

So often, the family of an alcoholic centers itself around the "problem," the alcoholic or addict. This creates an impossible situation— the family has made itself a hostage. Even though the family may pray and wait for the alcoholic to change, the focus is still on the problem.

This method rarely works even though prayer and patience are essential. We see that more is needed for a family to secure the common ground where we can live outside the bondage of addiction.

There are many tools you will need, many bits of wisdom you should have, and a willingness to do the right thing even when you don't feel like it. It is a battle for the life of the family that will not end. The serpent of addiction has bitten and its venom is a cunning foe.

As the alcoholic finds the desire to stay sober, so too must the family find the desire to be emotionally sober. Just as the affliction of alcoholism creates havoc in the alcoholic's life, the lack of emotional sobriety in the family creates destructive behaviors that affect the whole family.

Whatever the circumstances, however horrible the conditions, we urge you to keep an open mind and allow for change and healing even though it doesn't appear likely. It may seem at times that nothing is being gained. But patience will eventually pay off, and once committed, the family can work toward peace regardless of the problems. But know that your devotion to the process is essential. It won't always feel good and you may feel alone at times.

Here alas, is the rub. Are you personally committed? Will you give God another opportunity to perform a miracle in your life? Will you be willing to grow even though others appear lazy, even hostile?

If you are able to persevere one more time with God's strength, perhaps you can contribute something to the process you didn't know you had. This is the beauty of change within a family. It may start with any member who is willing to change and soon find fertile soil in others.

Hey, it's God...He wants to talk to you.

Welcome to Recovery

"He has so much potential, if he could just stay sober." We have heard this more times than we care to remember. Almost as popular is the mother who laments her son in prison by saying, "I know he has a good heart." Then we have the opposite perspective at times. "He'll never amount to anything!" or "He just needs to make up his mind."

Notice all of the moralizing that takes place. We long to make sense of it all. We blame the alcoholic, the family, society, circumstances, and plain old bad luck. We think we can find a solution if we can identify what caused the problem.

How wonderful it would be if this were only true. We call repairmen, tell them the symptom, they locate the problem, put in a new part and fix the problem. We may admit it is a little bit more complicated working through addictions in the family, but we try the same thing. The symptom is the alcoholic's bad behavior, the problem is he won't stop, he needs to put a "plug in the jug," and our whole family will be fine.

We then fix the broken alcoholic a few times, but he keeps breaking. He stays sober for a while but it doesn't last. We question what happened. Maybe we had the wrong therapist. Maybe he needs to go to a different 12-step group or a different church. Maybe he needs treatment again, or different treatment, or a change in scenery. Maybe his job is the problem, or his wife, or his childhood, or his self-esteem. Maybe, maybe, maybe!

Here's another maybe—maybe we need to quit making excuses and address the deeper problem. The issue here is that we have identified the alcoholic as the problem, whereas he is simply the symptom. The problem is usually a complex matrix of issues that include, among others, misperceptions of life, unrealistic desires, daily frustrations, genetics, learned behaviors, circumstances, and the delusion that God should give us what we want when we want it.

WOW! That is a lot to digest and the temptation may be to put this book down and look once again for an easier, softer way to make everything better. You will be tempted to fall back into your own power-less strategies because they are more familiar to you, and you reason that somehow, this time, maybe they will work because maybe the alcoholic is ready.

We may want to sit the alcoholic down, analyze their difficulties, develop solutions, get the family ready for change, remind everybody of what to do, and then hope and pray the process is successful. Loved ones seem to see the problem so clearly and think that the alcoholic could change if he only understood better, or if the alcoholic only knew how much he were loved, or if the alcoholic could only love the family more. But we are usually mistaken and often hopeful without good cause. It is good to be hopeful, but not good to be mistaken in our approach.

We might mistakenly assume the alcoholic wants to change and is capable of creating change in their life. He stayed sober once before and we cite that as evidence that he can change. Then we might be in-sulted or hurt if the alcoholic doesn't change after we have spent much time and money trying to help. We have given him our best and he con-tinues to ignore the obvious. Our own expectations and hopes eventually begin to suffer.

Even if we are fortunate enough to see self-knowledge and aware-ness sink deeply into the alcoholic, the truth is this information will not change the alcoholic's life. These inner awakenings are good, but unless they are accompanied by a deep spiritual commitment, these changes in consciousness are merely superficial. The alcoholic "sounds" like he is changing, and he is slightly, but these pieces of awareness often give the alcoholic and the family a false sense of confidence. Indeed, some alco-holics "think" they are getting better and then go about trying to prove they have command of their addiction.

Alcoholics often experiment, perhaps many times, to use their newfound wisdom to conquer their addiction, only to find that their ad-diction conquers them every time they try to prove otherwise. The entire family suffers when these little bits of progress don't translate into long-term gains. Families often throw their hands in the air and give up.

Here is where the family needs a revolutionary new approach. As the loved ones of a seemingly hopeless alcoholic, we will need to turn our efforts toward becoming a more effective support environment for a long-term sober lifestyle.

This will not be easy or simple. We may feel we are a good support system already. We reason that we should not have to put forth the effort since we are not the problem. We feel like we have done enough since we have given the alcoholic many chances to change. We feel cheated by God because we feel we don't deserve this situation. We often lose hope when we don't see changes that last. We want steady progress. This is where we need to adjust our thinking and prepare differently.

What we need to know, as the loved ones, is that change is a process, not a destination. The word "change" is an action verb primarily and not a noun. Change is not someplace you go, it is the process of going toward that place. Once you arrive, you will likely rest briefly and realize God is presenting you a new series of changes that will start leading you toward a still greater place.

Even when we don't see change, there is change happening. Sometimes the change is good, sometimes relapse happens. To make matters worse, our frustration becomes its own problem and we eventually find the need to affect some change just for our own sanity. Hard feelings may abound and the situation seems more hopeless and desperate than ever. Believe it or not, this may be good...extremely painful, even dangerous, but good.

Hopelessness is the beginning of change. Frustration fuels the desire for change. Desperation should be remembered and embraced as the motivation to create a system of love that will transform lives, not just the alcoholic's life, but also our own. It has been "all about the alcoholic" for far too long.

It is time for the family and loved ones to find a way to survive in peace. We will not ignore the problem but it will no longer dictate our feelings about life. We will invest the time to put the entire situation into perspective, discard our own misperceptions, and move forward in a way that will not only help us maintain peace, but will also serve as a beacon of light for the alcoholic to find peace in sobriety.

Welcome to recovery!

Here's the Cross Section of Families in Recovery...
Can you see yourself in there yet?

THe FAMily PHoto

The first funeral Farris preached was for a man he mentored who lost the battle for sobriety. Rick had started as no more than a boy with alcohol, quickly progressed to drugs, and eventually tried to overcome his addictive nature with proscribed pharmaceuticals that are designed to treat depression and anxiety.

Farris knew Rick for years and they worked on spiritual issues together, but Rick just couldn't seem to find relief anywhere he looked. Ruth worked with his wife, Kris, on their marital issues that seemed to almost constantly fuel a vicious cycle of frustration, family battles, and relapse.

During several years of "on again" and "off again" marital progress, Rick had resorted to leaving the home because he couldn't endure the battles on the home front. He found more peace staying holed up in a motel with a bottle and some prescription drugs. Kris couldn't keep from nagging him about things on a bad day, and on a good day she was still a constant reminder to Rick of his weakness. Rick was overly sensitive, would get angry and leave.

One time Kris called Farris and asked for help in locating Rick. Rick had left the home a few days earlier and she used caller ID on her phone to conclude that Rick was staying at a local motel. Kris was worried that Rick might need help because he had sounded desperate and Farris agreed to check on him. When Farris arrived he used the assistance of the motel manager to locate Rick and unlock the door after Rick didn't stir.

As Farris entered the room, he saw nothing but empty bottles and broken dreams. Rick came to and was startled. He hadn't expected to see Farris but quickly assessed the situation and series of events that led to his rescue. That would be the last rescue Rick would receive. Three months later, full of antidepressants and booze, he took his life.

Farris remembers one thing Rick said in the motel room that day, "Farris, I wish I had your faith." We cannot say if Rick ever came to accept life on life's terms, or if he ever found salvation. That is not our business even though it is always a concern, and simply put, we are glad not to be the judge of who is entered in the Book of Life. Our business is to help those who are willing and able to respond.

While there have been many success stories in our ministry, there is another couple we would like to discuss where the jury is still out. In the marriage of Dalton and Fran, Dalton was an alcoholic and also used a variety of pain medications that he accessed through his work in the medical field. Fran had a full-time job and had quit trusting Dalton to keep his word. This came after years of broken promises and lies, a female love interest on the side, and a long history of short bursts of sobriety followed by lengthier periods or relapse, guilt, sorrow and shame.

Both Dalton and Fran attended and are still engaged in evangelical churches that believe in the healing power of God. They spent years in worship going to the altar seeking blessings and hope, salvation and victory. They would live as overcomers for months on a pink heavenly cloud, only to have the peace disturbed by secretly slipping back into the old ways, eventually leading to public humiliation.

They have been confused as to why God doesn't seem to have answered their prayers. Why did Dalton continue to return to his secretive ways? How could Fran continue to have hope in their marriage? Why didn't the fervent prayers of the church suffice? Instead of going to the altar, why couldn't they find a way to live at the altar of their heart? Why couldn't their hearts reconcile and live in peace?

While these questions are easy to ask, there are no easy answers. Foremost we must understand that the cycles of addiction are deeply imbedded in both mind and body. While these fleshly bonds primarily reside in the alcoholic, they are the problem of the entire family. They are not born in isolation and they feed on a variety of issues and feelings within the alcoholic's entire social circle.

Sometimes a bad day at work might be to blame. Other times a harsh word at home could provide a trigger. In the final analysis, a broken shoestring could provide a breaking point. But the problem is not just the stressful situations; it is our lack of ability as a social unit to exhibit the kind of understanding that invites an alternative reaction to those stressers. Here is an example of how impossible it may be for a marriage to survive without an early and rapid response from a concerned spouse. Even then there are no guarantees.

Doug married a charming woman who liked to drink. Alcohol was a trivial and acceptable part of life. Over time, while Doug worked successfully and traveled, Dora became a resentful housewife without either of them even knowing it. Simply put, she missed having a real life of her own. Dora didn't really want to work, she just wanted to have some social connectedness and she found female friends who agreed. They went to restaurants where alcohol was served and the friends drank a bit more than they should at times. It seemed Dora was fine and Doug was glad she had something to do even though he wasn't entirely happy with Dora's choice of distractions.

Over time, Dora finally quit making dinner at home, became increasingly defiant toward Doug, and the bewildered Doug reacted forcefully in conversation to bring Dora back to her senses. Dora only resented Doug all the more because of him assuming a parental role in her life. She became an alcoholic rather quickly and started to develop relationships with other men she met outside the home environment. Doug and Dora saw that they were losing their life together but Dora couldn't stop herself. After several treatments and attempts at sobriety and renewed commitments to marital fidelity, the marriage was finally on the rocks.

Other situations arise in which a young son or daughter begins to experiment with alcohol or drugs. Within some family circles the parents encourage their children to "safely experiment" with alcohol use while in the home and under parental supervision. Setting aside the obvious legal and moral discussion, it is important to know how dangerous it is to allow teens to drink or use drugs, particularly if there is any history of alcohol or drug abuse in the extended family. You will see the whys and wherefores of the addiction-prone family circle later.

Let it suffice for now that parents often think of experimentation as harmless, but we need to beware. There are a clear percentage of individuals who react to alcohol and drugs differently from the vast majority of our population.

In at least 15% of the general population, the individual receives a noticeable benefit from their intake of alcohol or drugs, and any usage sets them up to crave more. The other 85% of the population has a different initial reaction. They start to feel a little odd and throttle back their usage so as not to lose control. Many young people who experiment with alcohol or drugs may fit in the group that quickly recovers control and avoids becoming obsessed, but at least 15% of them are going to find it difficult, if not impossible, to quit without a substantial investment of effort from them and the loved ones around them.

We have seen some parents bewildered that their child has become an alcoholic. The parents didn't encourage it, they may be religious and go to church, and there may not even be any obvious signs of any substance abuse in the family. It sometimes appears there is absolutely no reason for a person to become an alcoholic, but rest assured that the reason is there when we know how to look for it.

Even so, in the final analysis it is not important what causes any one person to be an alcoholic. It may or may not be helpful to have that information, but what is critical is to recognize the contributing factors in and around us.

Children who choose to escape reality are unhappy, nervous, and/or insecure. They are looking for something to make them comfortable. It will take very little encouragement for them to experiment with booze and drugs. If they are one of the 15% of the general population with the inherited genetic predisposition to enjoy a feeling of comfort from alcohol, their experiment will likely become their lifestyle. If they are part of the 85% who do not quickly fall in love with the feeling, they will either turn away from it or, if they are in emotional pain, push through their distaste for it and "power drink" their way to oblivion. In any event, they are needing to rid themselves of their emotional difficulties and will continue to try to find a way to do so.

Non-addictive personality types, also known as the 85%, might turn to rebellious music or lifestyles that scream out in some way. Their flamboyance may be condemned even though they are not using booze or drugs. Sometimes parents try to "correct" such youthful anomalies and may even unknowingly push them toward a counterculture that embraces drug and alcohol use. Other parents might make excuses for the unconventional behavior, expecting them to grow out of it. Those parents often fail to interact and assist their children in a critical time of their youthful life journey. These two types of parents are either abandoning their children by not engaging them, or engaging them in a forceful way that pushes them away.

Some youth come out of it when the parents lovingly work with them to help them find their way back, but most parents have little education about such things and ignore the problem until it is too late. Still other parents don't see it as a problem because they may also rely upon alcohol or drugs in order to feel better about life.

Sometimes the authorities get involved in raising our children and it becomes clear that we have waited too long as parents. We may be inclined to give up. We may console ourselves by saying, "After all, once they turn 18, they're on their own." Parents might then just bide their time and deal with calamities as they arise.

With adult alcoholics, change becomes more difficult because they mistake themselves for a mature adults instead of the disobedient children of God they have become. They think that their opinions are just as reasonable as the opinions of the sober people around them. While it isn't always the case, it could be that the other family members are equally disobedient to God.

Many families simply give up because there is nowhere to turn any longer. They seem to have exhausted their options. They may have encouraged their alcoholic to try treatments, medications and therapists, churches and 12-step groups, and they are dumbfounded that nothing seems to work. Yet they know that these methods appear to have worked for others. At this point they may have heard from people that the alcoholic "just isn't ready." They are left to wonder what is so different about this situation. What is the magic formula, the magic wand, or the magic pill?

When some families give up they try to contain the problem. They may avoid serving alcohol at family parties. They may gather a few family members together and isolate the individual for a stern talk or professional intervention. Eventually, many families quit inviting the alcoholic to family functions, choosing instead to stay clandestinely in touch with the alcoholic of the family. But, even after they have "given up," family discussion inevitably turns to address the obvious. What is wrong with our alcoholic and/or our family?

The Widow Johnson still hasn't made it to Al-Anon.

The Cycle of Addiction

Addictions begin with a desire for a better life. It may seem odd to say that, but many of our troubles start out with seemingly innocent desires.

How often have we bought something that we thought would make us feel better, only to tire of it and find a new desire? Perhaps we are restless or uncomfortable and want to distract ourselves from our discomfort. We might be experiencing some frustration in life, and none of us want to feel uneasy. So we consider what the problem is and look for a solution. That also sets us up as prospects for temptation. We desire to be comfortable.

So, desire is the first nudge in the flesh, but it is not the problem. Our natural desires are God-given instincts. We desire love, but we settle for sex. We desire to be respected and we settle for power. God approves of love and respect, but only when lived out in His holy ways.

We can't blame the desire. We must understand that our responses to satisfy those desires are what can be unholy. We need to look at our dilemma with God's eyes if possible. We might ask ourselves some questions.

Is our response appropriate? Has God given us some discomfort for a reason? Can we learn and grow spiritually from our discomfort? Or do we simply seek to get rid of the discomfort?

The first bad choice we make is to cave in to temptation. As innocent as this little bit of experimentation may be, this begins the addiction cycle. We failed to ask for the power to resist temptation. We let our desires control us instead of us controlling them.

To complicate things, temptation is not optional, it is everywhere. Even Jesus experienced temptation (Hebrews 4:15). Temptation first comes to us when we are innocent and impressionable. Even though the innocent is probably aware of the dangers of the temptation, like Eve in the garden, they have a desire for something more in life. Eve wanted to be wise like God (Genesis 3:6).

We all suffer from the desires of the flesh. We naturally want things we don't have. We see something that looks good and we go for it, not necessarily knowing what will happen, but curious and hopeful about the outcome. We may or may not have prayed about it.

The more we think about it, the more the temptation seems to grow. We build entire fantasies around what it will be like when we get the object of our affection. Then, when reality fails us, we may turn to the comforts of alcohol or other happiness substitutes to ease our disappointment. This can easily lead to substance and relationship dependence.

In the beginning of the addiction cycle nobody is considered an addict. The final hopelessness of an addiction may come quickly or slowly, but the story of addiction is the delusional hope for an easy solution to life's problems, an indulgence that will enhance our life. Initially, we don't expect our addictions to take over our lives, and for awhile they don't. Eventually they become regular practices, then habits, then horrible obsessions.

It is terrifying to watch as the alcoholic contributes toward his own decay, even to the point of destroying families and the lives of loved ones, strangely still claiming that he is not out of control. Some alcoholics are able to admit they have become addicted; others insist they can take it or leave it. They may even stay sober for a period of time to prove it, and experience feelings of being vindicated. They might pridefully say, "I told you I could stay sober. I just drink because I like it, I don't need it."

Alcoholics return to addictive behavior because there is still a perceived benefit available from the addictive substance. Once the body and mind are conditioned to rely upon the substance, a blind spot in the consciousness of the alcoholic develops to defend their self indulgence.

Many alcoholics honestly, yet delusionally, think that most people drink the same way they do. They think that it was "bad luck" that they got caught drinking and driving. They think the people around them are shrews who want to control them or prudes who don't know how to have fun. In some cases, they may be correct, but that fact becomes irrelevant as the alcoholic spirals downward.

During their downward spiral they are likely to be accused of being unable to control their drinking. Alcoholics then make it a point to engage their willpower as best they can to prove they are not alcoholic. Roger Ebert journalized, "The problem with using will power, for me, was that it lasted only until my will persuaded me I could take another drink."

In 12-step groups, the third-step deals directly with self will. People caught up in their addictions are said to be engaged in "self will run riot." The third-step requires that people turn their will and their life over to the care of God as they understand God.

That seems a reasonable request to make of somebody who has already lost control. Having been blessed by the curse of alcoholism, alcoholics must learn to allow God into their lives if they expect to live, and then they must make a choice every day thereafter to turn their will over to God.

As they start to feel better, they may take their daily willpower back from God. If they have been involved with other alcoholics in recovery they should recognize their obsessive thinking before they go off the deep end and take a drink. If they haven't the personal experience or friendships that will help them see the truth, they may well convince themselves that drinking is okay. They would then also tend to bulldoze those around them as they continue to engage their selfish will.

Eventually all practicing alcoholics become engulfed in remorse and demoralized because the benefit from the alcohol lessens and becomes blotted out by the consequences. It is just a matter of time. Once this happens, there is a window of opportunity and most alcoholics will find a period of sanity and sobriety before returning to their addiction. But the statistics are that 69% of alcoholics and addicts will fail to maintain a life of sobriety for even one full year. The prospects for a lifetime of sobriety are grim.

We may have heard the warnings in school, home and church, but it didn't seem like it applied to us. We might have wondered why, if alcohol is so dangerous, it is sold everywhere. On TV, we also see medications promoted constantly that promise to make things better. Life in today's world is largely bombarded with messages of instant gratification and easy solutions. Within the Robertson home, when we have a complex problem, sometimes we laughingly suggest, "We have a pill for that!"

Think back to the third grade when the teacher asked what children wanted to be when they grow up. Everybody wanted to be a fireman, nurse, policeman, mommy or teacher. Did anybody raise their hand and say they wanted to grow up and be an alcoholic?

No alcoholic knows exactly what will happen when they first drink or use drugs, no child knows the results of sexual immorality in advance, no bride envisions their charming moderate-drinking groom as a hopeless cause, no parent sees their baby girl as a pregnant runaway, and no gluttonous soul understood where they might end up before they started down the gluttonous path. We have no idea in advance how our little bit of self-indulgence can land us in dire straits. But eventually the signs on the path become clear and we start to see a pattern. Ultimately, you might recognize a potentially addictive personality type. They are people who can use up a year's supply of anything in just two weeks.

These addictive personality types might be problematic in a variety of areas and switch addictions over time as they increase in consciousness of each addiction. It is uncommon to see only one addiction over a lifetime.

This raises a question. Can the alcoholic drinker return to life as a normal drinker? Our suggestion is that a moderate drinker that once drank heavily in their life was probably never an alcoholic. We have seen many men die trying to prove they were not alcoholic, that they could moderate their drinking. This is death by pride and suicide on the installment plan.

A good metaphor for alcoholism is to think of the innocent casual drinker as a cucumber, fresh and green. It is picked and soaked in brine (alcohol) consistently over time and eventually becomes a pickle (alcoholic). Exactly when that cucumber became a pickle cannot quite be determined, but one thing is for sure...the pickle can never go back to being a cucumber.

There are people who would argue that being an alcoholic doesn't mean you can never be a normal drinker. This alone should be a signal. A nonalcoholic doesn't obsess over alcohol and spends little or no time planning on when or how much to drink. It isn't a major blip on their radar. People who happen to drink occasionally, even to excess at times, aren't necessarily alcoholic.

An alcoholic is somebody who has lost control. The famous author, F. Scott Fitzgerald, who died at age forty-four from a life of alcoholic excess rightly said, "First you take a drink, then the drink takes a drink, then the drink takes you."

This is the basic cycle of addiction. The frustrated man takes a drink and finds joy or relief from some stresser. The drink worked for him, so the success of drinking leads to another drink. The man tries to maintain that perfect high, but cannot do so for long. The alcoholic buzz is now trying to find its way back to that "sweet spot" where everything is fuzzy and good. It becomes an experiment in which the drink is the solution and the drinker is the laboratory. The sweet spot high is lost and cannot be found. Finally, in futile attempts to get back to that perfect high, the man loses himself in the bottle.

An alcoholic will sleep it off and try again another day, going through the same process. The inducement to drink is the "sweet spot" where life feels good. It will last sometimes for an hour or two, rarely more. The alcoholic is not addicted to the alcohol, they are addicted to the warm, fuzzy feeling that life is good. It just so happens that alcohol reliably takes them to that point and then drops them off, leaving them in bad neighborhoods of drunkenness where they can't seem to find their way back to that happy, warm, fuzzy feeling.

The lure to find that place is strong. Alcoholics will spend enormous amounts of time and money trying to control and enjoy their drinking, finally finding that there is no formula for the maintenance of the perfect high.

There are websites that discuss how to maintain the perfect alcoholic buzz by monitoring blood alcohol intake for your size and situation. Try as they may, there is no scientific formula to help somebody maintain the perfect high. The formulas can take many factors into account to try to help somebody take in just enough alcohol to maintain a steady high, but no formula exists that takes into account the body/brain chemistry and temperament of the individual.

That science belongs to God. He allows for a moment of perfect joy from time to time, but God doesn't want us to depend upon it, so He purposefully won't allow us to live in the stability of constant dependence upon alcohol. We are to live dependent upon His spirit, not the spirits.

But it starts out so innocently. That first little bit of self indulgence seems harmless. For most people it may be harmless. Even God says there is no sin in drinking, only in drunkenness. The problem comes when the harmless substance provides a benefit sufficient to cloud our better judgment.

A normal drinker might have a half glass of wine, push the glass aside and say, "I've had enough, I'm starting to feel it." An abnormal drinker would grab the glass and say to themselves, "Oh good! I'm starting to feel it."

The same paradigm can be applied to many things. People prioritize and often over indulge and make one thing more important, typically to the detriment of other things in life. So, what grabs your attention? It might be exercise, work, fast cars, romance, success, chocolate, food, sex, gambling, prejudice, or power. When we become drunk on power, are we not still drunk? The truth is we can be drunk on almost anything. More than once we have seen people overdose on church work!

While the goal for self indulgence is comfort, the outcome of taking comfort in an indulgence is not universal. Each person is different in their tolerance and their level of desire. While there are people who engage is some excess, still others become addicted. Here is the central theme—it isn't the substance/behavior that is the problem, it is our love of the substance/behavior. The little bit or relief it provides has seduced us into putting our worldly indulgence ahead of our spiritual sense of wellness.

We don't totally ignore God at these times. We just put Him on a shelf in our life and dust Him off when we need Him. Perhaps we pray to

Him twice a day as if He is some faraway czar of the universe. But the day to day fact is that we have sought to replace spirituality with something we can acquire and control and use to benefit ourselves, or at least we hope it turns out that way.

Let's face it. An alcoholic is a perfect example of relying on spirits instead of relying on the Spirit. It is easier to get relief that way, at least at first. You just can't run down to the store and buy a quart of Jesus... you have to romance your relationship with the Spirit of God and that is not easy to do when you are frustrated and angry. It's much easier to put your money on the bar and get some quick relief.

That is how it starts. Life's frustrations take hold. We fail to seek a godly solution. The frustrations turn to resentment and anger. Guess what is next?

The budding alcoholic takes a legal drink and gets a comforting feeling from it. The nonalcoholic takes a legal drink and feels a little odd and doesn't love it quite the same. The budding alcoholic then launches on a dubious avocation in alcoholism while the nonalcoholic decides the benefit doesn't interest them enough to continue down a path of alcoholic abandon. Of course, there are billions of varying degrees in between these responses, and there are hundreds of theories on why.

Most people manage their lives in moderation and cannot understand why other people cannot seem to exercise similar self control. If you are one of those people who don't understand why people drink or drug themselves into oblivion, take a few minutes in a little exercise.

Think of a language you do not speak and imagine yourself in a foreign country trying to have a conversation in that language. It is frustrating when you cannot understand a person who speaks a different language. You might even cleverly find a way to successfully communicate through gestures and sign, but you are still a stranger and cannot think in that foreign language. Instead, you think in your native language and reason out how to communicate those ideas and thoughts to the person who speaks the foreign language. You eventually find common ground once you work through the frustration.

So it is with communication between alcoholics and their nonalcoholic loved ones. The language of the heart of the alcoholic is based upon the unique perspective that alcohol or drugs provides a tangible benefit. The addicted heart isolates because the others don't understand. Also, the alcoholic doesn't expect them to understand. He knows that he has travelled down a road he wouldn't wish upon them.

In turn, friendly family members feel like they are in the middle of a foreign horror film, like dreamers in a nightmare they cannot comprehend. They cannot see the perceived benefit of alcohol to the alcoholic. They only see the havoc it creates.   The family and loved ones communicate their concerns but it doesn't make sense to the alcoholic because the alcoholic absolutely needs his alcohol. Communication is attempted many times, the ensuing arguments produce no resolution, and the situation leads to frustration for all concerned. Everybody tends to walk away discouraged, looking for a way to find peace despite desperate circumstances.

The alcoholic doesn't want to be treated differently, but creates the very estrangement he doesn't want. He feels he has no choice so he often leaves the family and seeks companionship elsewhere. He might even blame the spouse or other loved ones for his departure. He feels cut off and justified. Perhaps the alcoholic will find an understanding friend, perhaps even a new set of friends or a nonjudgmental member of the opposite sex.

The alcoholic's spouse and family are emotionally injured when the alcoholic's affections turn elsewhere. Family members eventually reach the point of not wanting the alcoholic in their lives, unless and until the alcoholic gets sober and repents of his ways.

The alcoholic will have a difficult time in his life where he has found no peace and lives in almost constant regret. He may have enjoyed some new friendships, but the new has worn off, the problems created by alcoholism have accompanied him everywhere he goes, and he thinks that maybe it is time to grow up, quit drinking, and return to the family.

The alcoholic may concoct a fantasy of a happy return as if he were the prodigal son returning to a jubilant family. Perhaps the alcoholic will instead hang his head, coming back humbly and impress his family that he has changed. In any event, the alcoholic might make these types of amends many times over before long-term recovery seems likely.

What is it that might work against a family that desires recovery? The alcoholic has likely been estranged for months, emotionally if not also physically. The family may be resentful instead of welcoming. They may only put on a good front because they don't expect the sobriety to last. Perhaps they have simply become burned out by the constant barrage of alcoholism in the past and were enjoying the peace of not having the alcoholic hurricane that seemed to constantly threaten their lives. Perhaps they have moved on emotionally and aren't ready to invest again in what they consider a losing cause.

Many family members may have these feelings and not even recognize them. If they even realize their feelings, it is unlikely the family will discuss this with the alcoholic because they love him and don't want to discourage him. However, they also don't want to become his hostage again. They might pretend to care, but not really put much effort into it.

They may be openly wary.

Other families might welcome the alcoholic back numerous times, always hoping and praying for healing and a new start in life for the alcoholic. They might create a hospitable environment for the alcoholic, invite him back into the home, and engage him in social activities, almost pretending that he hadn't been gone. Everybody knows the truth, but a family expressing forgiveness seems like the Christian thing to do and so everybody is urged to treat the alcoholic normally and give him a chance to show that he has changed.

What could possibly be wrong with either approach? The whole family desires the best, the alcoholic has returned with a repentant heart, and the family is hopeful. But the key question is, what has changed? Is there any evidence in communication that something has changed?

Many families are not geared up for success. The burned out family doesn't care to communicate and just waits to see if there has been a change in the alcoholic. They take a wait and see approach...time will tell. The welcoming family wants to communicate as if nothing ever happened. Let bygones be bygones...let's move on happily from here.

The problem in both cases is that they tend to ignore the need the alcoholic has to make amends to his family, not to mention his creditors, his job, and others. He might start to apologize and one family member might say, "Don't talk us through it, walk us through it!" Another family member might say, "Oh, don't worry about it, you just weren't yourself and we're just glad to see you back home."

While it may not sound like either response is inappropriate, there are better ways to create a healing experience. The family should be prepared, upon the return of the alcoholic, to meet him with a range of supportive methods, but just making it up as you go will not help. It will likely work against you. The family should have been preparing for this.

The alcoholic knows deep within they need to make amends but they may be too embarrassed to do so. If the family doesn't know how to handle communications and the alcoholic is still tender, the situation hasn't really changed, despite the fact that the alcoholic is sober for the moment. If family dysfunction was part of the problem for the alcoholic, then he has just returned to a source of frustration.

The family too can be frustrated. They are trying to react appropriately, but they just don't know what to do. Indeed, they may rather resent the fact that the alcoholic can breeze back into their life as if nothing was wrong. Something has to be said but nobody knows how to start the conversation.

While it would be nice if we could offer you a script for the return of the prodigal son, it would not be authentic. What will provide the best opportunity for the healing of the family that has been impacted by alcoholism is a healthy understanding of the nature of alcoholism, a willingness to contribute toward the common good, and the ability to be honest and loving at the same time.

But how can the family put aside their own hurt and anger time and time again?

Got a problem?

We have a pill for that!

THE ALCOHOLIC FAMILY

One of the most important concepts we must understand is that alcoholism affects the entire family. It is like one person who brings the flu home from school or work. We see one family member coming home sick and suffering, then the rest of the family soon gets sick. The Centers for Disease Control tell us that people react differently to the flu, and in alcoholism, different members of the family also display different symptoms.

Alcoholism wreaks a dozen different kinds of havoc. The drinker might be lying, spending recklessly, and avoiding the family. The nonalcoholics are often angry or depressed, and may also engage in deceit and manipulation as they struggle to insulate the family from the effects of alcoholism. The youth may become angry and feel deprived. They may start avoiding home where life is complicated by alcoholism. Everybody is likely to become more manipulative in order to survive and the family no longer has common ground from which to communicate. Suddenly, the whole family has been impacted by the ailment that was brought home by one person.

While the entire world seems to sit someplace between being in judgment of, or sympathetic toward, the alcoholic, notice that the focus is always on the problem, the alcoholic. It is so easy for us and the world around us to turn our attention to the most obvious issue. There are numerous treatment centers, programs, and meetings for the alcoholic. What help is available for the nonalcoholic loved ones?

The family needs help but usually doesn't realize it until the damage is severe. Then they turn to doctors, therapists, and often times psychotropic medications. The more fortunate family members may find the help they need before they start their own downhill slide.

Some live in shame and quiet desperation that becomes chronic depression. Others may join the alcoholic and lose their way with him. Some get medications and try to manage the experience emotionally with a minimal amount of therapeutic support. Some turn to find their own diversions that will please them. Some of those diversions are self-destructive and contribute toward the destruction of the family.

Notice that there are many different possible responses to the dilemma of the family and that these natural reactions do not offer any lasting relief. More fortunate families may see the family's difficulties starting and get the help they need sooner. They might contact a pastor for assistance or find a support group.

It takes a lot of courage to go to a spiritual authority and admit your family is broken and it takes still more courage to go to a public meeting where you will feel exposed. The temptation is to see a doctor instead, but few medical practitioners will refer you to healthy support groups, and fewer still will personalize the recommendation by giving you a phone number to call someone locally who could help. Medical practitioners are more likely to either medicate you or refer you to a mental health professional that may or may not be familiar with how to best help your family. Even so, doctors and therapists costs money and alcoholic families are often struggling financially.

Many times, a family is not emotionally prepared to admit they suffer from alcoholism. The most basic instinct is to deny that alcoholism is ruining their home. The family initially thinks of the drunk as a temporary situation. "He'll get over it" or "She's just going through a bad time" might explain a few days of behavior, but signs of drinking regularly must not be ignored or minimized.

Few families can recognize the early signs of alcoholism. They want to be optimistic. At first, they may be uncomfortable about the drinker's behavior but they don't want to confront the alcoholic for fear they may aggravate the situation. So, they monitor the situation rather than have a difficult conversation with the drinker.

Finally when they say something, the drinker may show remorse. The family then has their hope restored, at least momentarily. They are convinced they have diverted a disaster now that the alcoholic and family agree. It is easy to have hope at first when the alcoholic shows signs of remorse. In naïve hopefulness, the loved ones see the remorse as the alcoholic being repentant, but perhaps the alcoholic is really just embarrassed or ashamed.

At this point, the alcoholic may cut back a little bit and the family is content that they are back on track. They have put aside any concerns for the moment even though they may keep an eye on the situation.

When the alcoholic exhibits more symptoms, the family becomes more concerned, but they still see the problem as strictly being within the domain of the alcoholic. The alcoholic is the one that spent the grocery money on booze. The alcoholic is the one that made a scene at the company Christmas party. The alcoholic is the one that was arrested for driving while under the influence. The alcoholic is the one that fails to keep important family commitments.

The family might finally see that the alcoholic is not just a problem drinker. Perhaps they have researched the subject and concluded their loved one may well be an alcoholic. This is likely the family's first step in overcoming their own denial.

Family members still may not see the impact alcohol abuse is having on the family morale, but at least they have quit pretending there is no problem. At this point the family itself has not become demoralized enough to seek assistance for their own sake and will likely be focusing on the alcoholic.

The family's denial grows deeper as they are finally relieved that they have now identified the problem...they have a real alcoholic on their hands! Now they can focus on helping that alcoholic family member. But they reason they may have to be careful in doing so. They wouldn't want to push the alcoholic away and see him get worse. So the family engages in secretly trying to "help" the alcoholic.

The spouse may call work for the alcoholic and explain that the alcoholic is too sick to come to work when he really has a hangover. The family may assist with court costs, take a job to help pay family bills, remind the alcoholic of important calendar events that he has started to forget, or perform the household chores that used to be handled by the alcoholic.

The family may reason that their kindness toward the alcoholic will be appreciated and recognized. They hope the alcoholic responds positively toward their generous efforts. At this point they don't realize the alcoholic probably doesn't even notice.

Now, the family is no longer denying the problem, but they still perceive the alcoholic as an able participant within the family instead of a handicapped person living in the home. The family is still in denial of their condition even though they have become aware of the alcoholic's condition.

What the families of alcoholics don't see is that they also have symptoms. While symptoms of the alcoholic include financial irresponsibility, physical infirmities, and emotional somersaults, the symptoms of the family include embarrassment of the past, fear of the future, the inability to stay in the moment, fatalistic thinking and a loss of hope.

Over time, the alcoholic will become less and less able to maintain their commitments in life because they spend more time considering when and how much they will drink. Other priorities fade as alcoholism increases.

Alcoholics will normally work hard to maintain their façade of full functionality in order to avoid confrontation. There will probably even be some improvements in the situation. Alcoholism is not often a condition that only worsens. It tends to ebb and flow with changing circumstances and perceptions. Positive events will often help the family pretend that alcohol intake is just part of life. They will forget about their past dilemmas and live the good life while it is available. Unfortunately, alcoholism is a cunning and patient adversary.

The permissiveness of the family during good times may lend the mistaken impression to the alcoholic that drinking is okay, that moderation is a relative term, and that drinking in excess is something the family may tolerate from time to time.

As the beast of alcoholism returns and destroys the memories of the previous good times, as the family's gestures of goodwill go unnoticed or unappreciated by the alcoholic, and as the alcoholic drinks more to find a selfish level of alcoholic comfort, the family becomes more discouraged but still lives in denial. They continue to see the alcoholic as the only problem even as they themselves start to become part of the family problem.

Al-Anon Family Groups is a 12-step fellowship where the family and friends of problem drinkers come together and share their experience, strength and hope. Teenagers in the Al-Anon Family Group program, Alateen, often report that they prefer to deal with the alcoholic rather than the family. Once the family starts to exhibit their own unhealthy symptoms, the teens find that predicting the mood of the alcoholic is easier than predicting the reactions of other family members. The teens also report being able to know when to approach the alcoholic to get the things the teen needs to survive, an essential goal at times when the rest of the family is living with feelings of deprivation and hostility.

Spouses feel deprived of love...they see the alcoholic putting alcohol and drinking opportunities ahead of them and the family. They see the family's finances squandered. They start to imagine scenarios where the alcoholic is being unfaithful in more way than one. The alcoholic is obviously the problem to them and they dwell on that problem increasingly.

During the good times they are still sometimes able to feel real affection toward the alcoholic even though the alcoholic may be drinking. They still see the excess of alcohol as the problem and try to help the alcoholic control their drinking. They are hesitant to admit they are married to an alcoholic because they think the alcoholism also reflects on them... as if they helped create it. No doubt in many cases they have contributed.

Spouses may also resent other family members or friends making remarks about alcoholism or the marriage. Their defensive posture is a very clear warning sign that they are deep in denial. Even though their hope for the return of their healthy spouse seems increasingly more distant, they can become like a beggar looking for table scraps of affection from the alcoholic, accepting any kind words or positive acts as indicators that things are getting better. This person, because of their ongoing willingness to overlook the obvious, is likely to show signs of melancholy. They are grasping at straws and when they finally lose hope, they are likely to become emotionally paralyzed and fall into depression.

The opposite can also be true. There are spouses who prematurely cut off the alcoholic from any opportunity to drink or squander family resources. They may take charge of the checkbook and credit cards and control any cash in the possession of the alcoholic. They may search the house, car and alcoholic's personal belongings for any signs of substance abuse or infidelity. They may mark the bottles of alcohol in the house to monitor alcohol usage or they may throw the booze away.

This spouse may eventually become like a parent to the alcoholic. But even for the "take charge" type, the alcoholic is still "the problem" and they will not likely see that they are every bit as codependent and hopeless as the melancholy spouse who cries out for love. They are two sides of the same codependent coin. The alcoholic is the problem and they think they can be part of the solution by managing the situation better. Their goal is to get the alcoholic to change.

At this point, the reader may say, "Of course that is their goal and that is also my goal!" Please remember that having that as your primary goal is a sure way to feel like a failure. Instead of the sobriety of the alcoholic being the goal, the sobriety of the alcoholic may prove to be an outcome. The goal for the family should be to live a successful, fruitful life whether the alcoholic is sober or not.

The loved ones of the alcoholic have tried so many things to get the alcoholic sober it is surely difficult to move their focus to anything else. Everything has centered on "the problem" and our activities revolve around becoming a better support system for the alcoholic. Many become dedicated to understanding alcoholism and finding the solution to get their alcoholic loved one sober.

They often read self-help books about alcoholism, they may put alcoholic literature around the house for the alcoholic to discover, they may invite sober friends to the house, but they all engage in some form of family management in an attempt to create an artificial environment that will facilitate the alcoholic getting sober. When nothing seems to work they give up, only to find a shred of new hope, try again, and fail again. At some point, somebody in the family is going to break down and it may not be the alcoholic.

When the spouse and family reach this point they are in crisis. Reality has set in. Family survival is now at issue. Finally, the family is on the verge of self recognition of their denial. They have moved past the hopeful stage, engaged the family, and undoubtedly began a family conversation.

By this point, they may have given up questioning the alcoholic, they may have given up searching for booze, and they have likely given up tracking the movements of the alcoholic. These are all good signs that the family is realizing they are powerless over the alcoholic's folly. But they should never give up on the family and maintaining a healthy home, despite the absence or presence of the alcoholic or whether the alcoholic is still drinking or sober.

Nonalcoholics have tried to save the family through secrecy, manipulation of circumstances, or engaging in aggressive behavior, all to no avail. These efforts typically do nothing but fuel the drama that has already started to destroy the family. Perhaps now the family is ready for a real solution: a solution based upon honest self-evaluation and communication.

Many loved ones think they have been doing a good job of communicating and holding the family together. Even if this is true, there is always a need to delve deeper, to consider motives and processes carefully, and to constantly monitor our approach toward those who live with us. This is when our eyes can start to turn inward and find solutions.

The loved ones must leave "no stone unturned" in saving the family since they will likely be working on that with little or no help. Indeed, the first thing the family must do is make sure they have not become part of the system of self destruction. Look carefully at your behaviors.

Behavior doesn't lie. It is the most accurate portrayal of what we communicate. This is true for the whole family.

Just after a horrible alcoholic spree disrupts the peace, many families have heard the alcoholic pathetically claim how much he loves them. Then the family is likely to say, "If you loved us, you wouldn't drink." His words don't impress the family when his behavior communicates chaos. But the family also miscommunicates and compounds the drama.

Many spouses tell the alcoholic they would do anything to help, but then might complain they can't be affectionate with the alcoholic because their feelings are hurt. Perhaps the family engages in unhelpful behaviors such as pouting, slamming doors, yelling, or maintaining an angry silence. Perhaps they instead try to be constructive and plot together to keep the alcoholic sober.

Look carefully at these situations and consider what is being communicated. Holding back affection, acting out, or orchestrating situations to ensure sobriety are behaviors that speak louder than words. The alcoholic, when the family is misbehaving, is not experiencing the support the family claims to offer. The alcoholic is then likely to become angry as he thinks the family only wants to either punish him or control his behavior. It is safe to say that increasing drama fuels alcoholism throughout the home.

Children can also be part of this pattern of miscommunication. They may not want to admit they are so severely impacted by the crumbling family, or they may not even be aware of their feelings. When asked how they are doing or how they feel about the alcoholic, they might honestly answer they love the alcoholic and want to help him change. But their behavior may not match. They might stay away from home more, lock themselves in their room, or act out negatively to try to get some much needed attention. Again, the mismatch between words and actions.

Our words are coming out of our mouths and expressing how our heart might look in a perfect world, but we live in a situation full of decay. Ultimately, our actions will betray us. We even act against our own verbalized desires though we hate to admit it.

Some of us think good communication is "in your face," or a well-timed silent treatment, or a family intervention that puts the alcoholic on the "hot seat." Honestly there could be a time for any of these, but not one of them is of any value until we have taken the time to identify our motives and prepare for effective communications.

So, what makes a communication effective? Effective communication is communication that connects us to others instead of disconnecting us from others. It closes the space between us and the person with whom we seek to communicate. It is that simple.

We will be discussing this in some detail but an easy example can be found in how *we handle* a feeling of anger. It is effective to express that anger and there are many ways to do so. It is more effective if, when shared, the person can understand our point of view. It is less effective if we judgmentally rant, but it is still effective because we have created a connection even though it isn't a happy one.

It is ineffective communication if we just bottle it up or do something secretly vengeful. We then haven't communicated anything. All we have done is blown off steam. So, for now, let's make sure that we understand that effective communication is an honest exchange, but not necessarily something that will result in quick and happy results.

Usually we have to have some difficult conversations to become good at effective communication. But the good news is that we are finally on the road to getting connected again. Good communication is the path to mutual appreciation, and mutual appreciation helps us survive the storms.

To more fully appreciate the importance of good communication and how it leads to feelings of unity and connectedness, first we should consider the origins of our feelings of disconnection and how it has affected not just us, but all of mankind.

Say what you mean, and mean what you say,
but don't say it meanly.

"If we're going to make it as a couple,
we need one rule: No Dancing."

How Far We Have Fallen

Whatever might be your belief about the timeline for the creation of earth, allow yourself to consider the perfection of the Garden of Eden. Before the fall of mankind we enjoyed perfect unity with God. We walked in the garden with God and enjoyed the wholesome perfection of His creation. We were fully connected, completely at peace, and satisfied. We were so perfect in our vision of life and one another that we existed in oneness, not even aware that we were unclothed. In other words, there was no shame, no guilt, and no sin.

Then came the cunning creature, the snake, engaging Eve in conversation. Her first mistake was entertaining the discussion.

Every good parent tells their children to beware of strangers, yet children are still drawn by sad strangers who are looking for missing pets or seemingly helpless strangers who are lost. In Genesis 3:1 (NIV), the snake asks a seemingly harmless question about what instructions God gave them about the trees in the garden: "Did God really say you couldn't eat from any tree in the garden?"

Eve then defended God and told the serpent how willing God had been to share everything good with them. As she was sharing, she made sure she mentioned the rule wherein God had warned them about the tree in the middle of the garden.

Draw a comparison to a child being questioned by a stranger. The stranger might manipulate the child by asking, "Are your parents afraid you will get lost if you help me find my lost little puppy?" The child wants to be helpful and isn't sophisticated enough to see the ploy. The child doesn't want the friendly stranger to think badly of the parents nor encourage the stranger to doubt his parents. The child also can't see the evil of the stranger questioning the wisdom of the child's parents. Children simply don't think of evil. Furthermore, the child wouldn't want it to appear that his parents raised children who were uncaring or otherwise unhelpful. Add to all that the lure of being a hero to a poor lost puppy!

In Eve's case, she didn't want to appear weak and she didn't want to admit that she would like to be wise like her Father. Perhaps she thought her Father didn't know how capable she was of handling things. So, when the serpent pointed out the parent surely must be wrong, she wanted to believe the lie.

Likewise, a child confronted by a stranger might not want to believe their parents could be wrong. The child might also assume that his overprotective parents are needlessly worried and that they tend to underestimate his abilities.

Once the child has crossed that seemingly minor threshold of disobedience, the child is now free to dwell on becoming the hero that saves the lost little puppy. Once Eve decided she could disobey God and it wouldn't hurt anything, she set aside her concern and then focused on the forbidden fruit. She wants that wisdom. Perhaps she thinks it must be good if God is keeping it to Himself. Her pride in becoming wise like the Father takes over. Finally she sins and thereby sets up the enduring battle between the flesh and the spirit.

The very next generation is warned about this ongoing battle. God tells Cain in Genesis 4:7 (NLT), "Sin is crouching at the door, eager to control you. But you must subdue it and be its master." We then read that Cain murdered his brother Abel because Cain was resentful toward God and Abel. He decided to make his own rules of what is right.

Eve believed the lie of the serpent, her son Cain created his own lies, and in one generation mankind moved from disobedience to murder. Hundreds of generations later we like to think we have improved, but an honest self appraisal of the human condition will show we are only more sophisticated. We are doomed to self consciousness instead of childhood innocence.

After our sin in the garden, we immediately saw our own nakedness and became acutely aware of our newly perceived imperfections. We were no longer going to be allowed to dwell like children, laughing and playing and living off the land, experiencing that warm, confident feeling that is the evidence of the presence of God in our life. We now had worries, and it got worse over time.

Once sin was inherent in the human condition, we no longer had a single, simple, natural godly path. Now we had to choose constantly between the perfect spirit of peace and the powerful feelings of flesh that we had just started to experience. Without going into the entire history of mankind, if you have read Noah's story, you can see which way it went.

Today, we are each wearing six thousand year old flesh. We have inherited a sophisticated and decadent sin nature that has adapted and lost its way. Now we find ourselves living in the seventh millennium as if there is no God. We can create clones, spare body parts, visit outer space, and keep people alive longer than ever since the early days after the fall of man. But what have we gained?

Despite all of our technological advances and sophisticated life-styles we are still being defeated by an age old scourge of man, the simple little grape! Truly, we should be embarrassed that we haven't been able to conquer alcoholism.   For all of our accumulated knowledge, we still barely understand the human mind and how it works.

One year we tout one idea, the next year another, perhaps even the opposite. As a society we are not much different than the alcoholic, grasping at straws, foolishly proud of ourselves and our progress as a civilization.

Our tendency is to grab at things that make us feel better quickly. We reach out for counterfeit comforts, ignoring the seemingly complex spiritual work that might resolve our core issues. Rather than search for the inner peace that will satisfy us, we treat the symptoms and are elated when it happens to work.

How many times has a friend bragged about some new solution in their life? A new diet or exercise fad or music craze or TV show gives us a way to set aside our more difficult life issues. It is easier to take a drink, proscribe a pill, or find a diversion rather than seek a spiritual solution for our seemingly complex dilemmas. We race to find things that will comfort us, and we put aside concerns that our self indulgence is likely to create still more complications over time. Our moral compass seeks peace but it has been compromised by the desires of the hungry heart, and the counterfeit comforts of life become our poor substitute for God's peace.

Naturally, every person desires to avoid emotional pain and experience comfort, so we needn't be harsh on ourselves. Those who say pain is good, such as masochists, just have an alternative viewpoint of what is painful or comfortable. People will always go to great lengths to experience comfort while they hope to find peace. That process starts for each of us at the beginning of life.

Imagine yourself in heaven in the bosom of God long before you were born. You are surrounded in perfect light and warmth. You are being created and prepared for life. Your spirit is perfectly at peace with God as He reproduces a little piece of Himself and gives you a soul.

He assigns you a wide array of talents and character traits that make you unique. He knows you are going into a life form that has been corrupted by evil, but He also knows He will be there with you, inherent in your very conscience, waiting to be called upon to help His precious child thrive.

Someday He hopes to see you return, wiser and more like Him. That is a wonderful way for God to grow His family. Like a good parent, He wants you to experience life and make good decisions, but He knows that only an independent life can make decisions. So, your Loving Father gives you independence by wiping your consciousness of heaven clean from your mind and giving you a human experience in the flesh.

So then, can we now agree that we are not human beings striving for a spiritual experience in life? Rather, we are spiritual beings having a human experience. We carry God's spiritual DNA with us even as we are knit within our physical form and birthed into a worldly family.

So we come into the world with a child's perfect spirit but man's corrupt DNA of the flesh. This is the beginning of our living freedom. Here we will start to make choices. Can we dwell in spiritual perfection in this new place? That was the original plan. In fact, it is still the plan for us.

Jesus plainly said and every Gospel author clearly made this point: We must turn away from sin and become like children to enter the Kingdom of God. The writer of Hebrews refers to God as the Father of Spirits, and undoubtedly we are included as His spiritual offspring. The question becomes if we are willing to acknowledge our Father.

Imagine now that you are a child in the womb, in perfect peace, reliant on the mother, well fed, warm and comfortable. You are now in transition from God's bosom to the world. The perfect incubator for the transition is your loving mother. Your first consciousness as an embryo is your last consciousness of heaven. There is no turning back.

You are warm and enjoy your mother's steady heartbeat, the constant nourishment, the increase in physical sensations. You have an awareness that you are a separate being as you experience some squirming and feelings. It is a fuzzy, comfortable world in which you live, but things eventually start to change.

Up to now, you haven't wanted for anything, but you are experiencing a stirring in your flesh. You don't know it but you are in the third trimester and you need to let your mother know that it is getting close to time. You roll around, wrestle and kick a little.

In another month you experience the need to break free...like a baby chick breaking through the egg you push your head toward the birth canal. You kick and see and hear better than ever and your strength is amazing to you. You start to squirm to find the way out.

Suddenly, the watery comfort disappears and your agitation increases. You experience no cushioning and start to kick and push harder. The light increases as you readjust your body to escape. Suddenly there is a light brighter than you have ever seen. It is scary and wonderful and you are obligated in your spirit to break free.

There is some help coming from outside and you panic slightly. You know you are on the verge of something huge! You struggle as you are being pushed and pulled, then a blinding light and cold air produces startling new sensations. You don't know if you have been captured by enemies or been freed from confinement. Confusion reigns as you are manhandled and hanging upside down.

Bright light and feelings of being exposed consume you. Your blood is pumping hard! Everything is bizarre and you don't know up from down. You are more helpless than you have ever been. Fear grasps you as you realize you are supposed to breathe. Somebody slaps you on your bottom and you feel it and hear it and react. You start crying as loud as you can. HELP ME! You keep crying for several minutes as you are tossed to and fro. You are probed, poked, pricked, rubbed down and wrapped up.

Finally, you hear something and feel something familiar. You are back with your mother! Wow, what an experience that was! What could be next?

Congratulations, you've been born! From this point forward, try as we may, there is no turning back. God has put us upon the earth to live.

The ways we try to revisit our peaceful and comfortable place change over time. The breast is a soon and sudden comforter. The heart-beat and the soothing words we hear all help settle our nerves. Then we learn to cry out when we are hungry, thirsty, or lonely. Then we learn to cry out for other stuff. We find out we can get rid of an uncomfortable diaper. We can get a toy. We can escape the crib they have us in.

Once we get out and away from Mom, we start to look around and make decisions. Little boys often like Mom and learn to emulate Dad. Little girls like the attention they get from Dad and learn to emulate Mom. We develop strategies at an early age that work to get the things we think we need.

As years go by we become more sophisticated in our ploys to achieve our creature comforts and most of us learn to cooperate in order to gain the things that please us. Some of us find that we can get satisfaction sooner if we are willing to take short cuts. We are manipulative with-out even being conscious of it. We just naturally grab for things we want.

We are now a part of the human condition. Each of us brings our own complex myriad of genetic tendencies and God-given talents and character. Is it any wonder we are all different? Yet our desires and methods of pursuit are all so similar. That makes it easier for commercial geniuses to create counterfeit solutions that will capture our attention and comfort large numbers of people.

As individuals have sought more and better creature comforts over the centuries, entrepreneurs in society have worked to sell us these comforts.   Alcohol and drugs are two large examples among many. Decadent counterfeits and sin abound.   We have counterfeit marriage, decadent sex, gluttonous living, human trafficking, cloning, Hollywood idol worship, deep cravings for personal power, and cosmetic body development.   We are a phony people who have turned away from God and sought comfort wherever we can find it.   We have decided that God is no longer a reliable source for comfort and so we seek the counterfeit alternatives.

The peace we had in heaven when God created us is long gone. We are fully engaged in a world of conflict, where lip service is given to the concept of world peace as everybody pursues the things they think they need to survive and thrive.   We have become human beings instead of spiritual beings.   Our hope for anything spiritual is diminished and far away.   The closest we may come to getting spiritual now is something that makes us comfortable.

At the family level, think about how much easier it is for an alcoholic to get spirits than it is to get spiritual.   We see there are many counterfeit comforts being sought, but how does this impact us and our families?   What are the final results of our self seeking ways?

Across the board, mankind is more sophisticated, living better and longer and able to do a better job of supplying our own needs.   We have spare body parts, genetic food, and cloned animals.   Still, even though we have more and live longer, we are still desperate for peace.   We cannot seem to find the embryonic calm we once enjoyed within God's bosom.

The essence of the issue is simple.   We can have a full stomach and still suffer from an empty heart.   We can help others in ways that are sacrificial and still not experience the joy of that giving.   Unless we find a way to be in unity with the Creator and be creative in His perfect ways, the substitutes we develop will always fall short of our peaceful goal.

The world full of packaged spirits cannot compete with the Free Spirit that calls us out to greatness.   Our willingness to settle for less and our acceptance of mediocrity is the cursed way we prefer to live.   It is just easier for us, or so we think.

The base issue is that we do not know how to experience ourselves in the way God created us.   We are magnificent spiritual beings overcome by the desires of the flesh and the ways of the world and have forgotten the ways of our Heavenly Father, our very Creator.

So, we all know that somehow we need a spiritual solution, and yet we don't know how to go about it.   We all know it has something to do with relationships and communication, but we don't know how to proceed.   We all feel disconnected, like we are looking at life through our own blindness, yet this is the only pair of eyes we have.   How can we move back to being connected and feeling the Spirit of Life? What is the process of creating peace?

We are often in a hurry and don't know which way to turn. Looking for the outward road signs doesn't always work.

The Need to Feel Connected

Sin results from looking for love in all the wrong places. We want to return to the feelings of peace we experienced when we were comfortably in the bosom of God, but don't know how. Since the fall we have sensed ourselves as separate from God, and also perceived how we are different from the people around us. It is rather confusing for us and we experience loneliness, sometimes even in a crowd.

Many of us may feel inferior to others and unsuited for success. We try to compensate and achieve success in our endeavors. Most of us won't realize we're in trouble until God allows failure to destroy our carefully self-constructed realities. Our isolation and anxiety is increased.

We may put on forceful brave faces and attempt to dominate or control our existence. Others may cave in and try to hide from life. However we choose to react to adversity in our lives, to be fair, we all suffer with some anxiety over our being disconnected. You can call it an attachment disorder if you like, but the universal problem is quite basic. We try to find something that will comfort us, something that will take us back to the feelings of peace and perfection.

While we may intuitively know that we should seek spiritual strength to find peace, instead we rely upon the ways of fleshly comfort because they seem more reliable. We take the easier, softer way even though we know better.

Ecclesiastes 3:11 tells us that God has set eternity within our hearts. In Romans 2:15 we see that mankind has the laws of God written on our hearts and in our conscience. It is quite clear that God is present and accounted for if we will turn toward that inner truth instead of seeking satisfaction in the outward ways of the flesh.

So, while we have no excuse for ignoring the truth of God, still we find it extraordinarily difficult to live in the power of that truth. Instead of putting our confidence in that truth and waiting for God's blessings to come upon us, we put confidence in the things of the world and pretend that they are good enough for us. Simply put, our hope is misplaced.

Personally speaking, as a husband-wife team, we have counseled with married couples who want to separate. Couples have often reached the point of saying the love is gone or they never really had it. They often say they should have never married. That tells us their hope was in the feelings of love all along. We would point out here that feelings are not facts, and feelings need to be tested against the word of God.

It is common for people to live in the delusions of their feelings. Early in romance people are often hopelessly in love and think that romance is the basis of the ongoing relationship. As the honeymoon and the romance wears thin, they realize they are in trouble. They might try a variety of things to invigorate their marriage. Some of those things might excite them and renew their romantic feelings, but they are still founded in the delusion of romance. The problem is the basis for the relationship is romance.

To add longevity to romance requires more than a feeling because there will always come a time when the roller coaster of life will work against even a healthy relationship. We need to realize that God uses romantic feelings to first draw two people together, and while romance may be the first cause of a relationship, it is not the basis for an ongoing healthy relationship.

Consider that God uses romance to propagate the earth. We know that romance and sex go together and thus we populate the earth. That is simple enough for us all to agree.

It is then up to the man and the woman to grow past romance and into relationship. They must allow their commitment to each other to take priority over their feelings about each other. This is the sign of a mature marriage.

As children become part of the equation, we see how God uses our fleshly romantic feelings for our spouse, along with our increasing spiritual commitment for family and children, to continue to grow and mature us. God is ultimately all about unity and commitment. Feelings may entice us toward things, good and bad alike, but they are not meant to be our sustenance.

In 1 Corinthians 13, also known as the Love Chapter, Paul describes himself as having once been a child who spoke and thought as a child. When he became a man, he put away childish things. Romance is the childish part of love...it isn't bad, it is just not perfected. The perfection of love is in self sacrifice, and people who live on feelings are selfish, not sacrificial.

So, when we personally counsel a couple who complain they have lost their love together, the truth is that they have lost their romantic delusion and have not yet grown up together in sacrificial love. One or both of them are acting selfishly.

Sometimes one partner in a marriage may be under the impression that they are acting sacrificially in the relationship. Perhaps this will be partially true, but usually a person who thinks they are being a martyr has not yet become conscious of their latest challenges. There is always a way to be more like Christ.

Perhaps a couple are no longer romantic lovers, perhaps the wife has become the mother toward the disobedient man-boy, or the husband becomes the father to a delinquent wife, perhaps they have become "friends" and quit being allies or lovers. They don't know who they are together any longer. They may feel they have lost their common point of view whereas they probably never had a significant common mission in life. Romance may have been their only common thread.

But God is not to be mocked. We believe that romance was meant to bring a couple together and, over time, mature in love. God often brings together impossible opposites and gives them a desire to work it out. We like to think our own marriage is a testament of God's power to do so.

On a personal note, when we met, Ruth was a female, Jewish non-believer, Democrat, liberal. Farris was a male Christian, Republican, conservative. Ruth didn't believe in corporal punishment and Farris did. The differences went on and on.

We surely had our difficult years, but we stuck it out. Now we look back and see that we each had to be willing to do what was right for the marriage. The marriage was ordained by God. It was not for us to set that aside for any selfish reason.

That meant we had to be sacrificial. As things have worked out, nowadays we have learned a great deal about each other's perspectives and we can lovingly (on most days) discuss a large array of delicate and difficult topics because we are experienced in trusting God to lead the way. Also, without disclosing which way things have gone politically or economically, we want you to know that our individual perspectives are irrelevant and our unity in approach is essential. We have become the allies that God wanted us to be and are in the middle of the mission He proscribes.

It could have gone another way. Either of us might have given up somewhere along the way, but we were blessed with tenacity. The same stubbornness we sometimes used against each other had become a way for us to stay steadfast in our marriage, despite the difficult years. Because we each worked on ourselves first, because we put truth ahead of our feelings, we have managed to survive. We have subjugated our feelings for the higher goal of unity in the marriage.

Living by one's feelings is like being a leaf in the wind. Some poetic souls may find comfort in constantly yielding to the feelings of the flesh, but the flesh is a cruel master. Just ask the alcoholic who cannot keep from taking a drink as he tries to quench the fire burning inside him. Does it work?

Pouring booze down our throat to drown our sorrows is like pouring gas on a fire to put it out. We are so hopeful we will get the result we want that we will likely dismiss any evidence to the contrary. The alcoholic, in a desire to feel better, will pour gas on the fire and not notice the blazing inferno in and around him. All that matters is his false sense of comfort, that his mind is numbed for the moment.

In turn, the wife who constantly waits by the phone or waits to hear the car pulling into the driveway is also pouring gas on the fire. She longs to have the home fires lit for the alcoholic, thinking he will one day come to his senses. Her desire for him to behave the way she wants seems a reasonable expectation to her. She doesn't see that she is spiraling out of control by heaping the fuel of unreasonable expectations upon a man who cannot respond. Her fire is the delusion of a perfect life and she keeps fueling it despite the deteriorating circumstances.

Whether husband or wife, alcoholic or codependent, we have finally become disconnected from reality. We may still wake up and bathe and eat and go through the motions of life, but we are starting to die in our spirit. We have put the world ahead of God and it is taking its toll upon us. So, there it is. The final disconnect is the disconnection from reality.

Call it neurosis, psychosis, or hypnosis, we prefer the delusional world we have begun to create. We are now lost inside our feelings and grasping at straws, rejecting those aspects of life that don't fit our world view.

This may seem extreme, and it is. So, shall we see just how far down the road of delusion we can travel without hitting the final "disconnect" of insanity? Self indulgent thinking is the first step down the wrong road. Few will fully disconnect, but millions will play with the fire and hope to keep it under control.

When the fire starts to blaze out of control for alcoholics, they end up in treatment centers, jails, hospitals, car wrecks, and funeral parlors. The nonalcoholic loved ones may not have the same publically humiliating outcomes, but their inability to control their circumstances leads them to therapists, depression, divorce, medications, selfish isolation, outside sexual relationships, inappropriate displays of anger, and sometimes suicide or homicide.

The other alternative to managing our feelings is to recognize them and not act out. Sometimes doing nothing is the most you can do. If you can be sensitive to your desires and recognize your secretive thoughts, if you can project their potential for danger, then we can ask for God's help in overcoming them. Otherwise we will likely lose control and become enslaved by those feelings, acting out without even knowing it.

How to Reconnect

We long to be at peace and comforted by God. It is interesting that Jesus (John 14) refers to the Holy Spirit as the Comforter. As believers, we are promised that the Comforter is with us forever. Yet, the call of our flesh is so strong and the demands of day-to-day living so great, the voice of the Comforter can be drowned out by our own selfish desires and the clamor of the world around us.

The patience required for us to achieve a satisfying relationship with the Comforter seems too difficult. The Comforter can't be summoned by us at will and we turn away from God to the ways of the flesh automatically. We don't necessarily make a plan to sin. It just seems like a reliable way to get the comfort we feel we need.

What can we do to get reconnected when it seems so far away? The key to being wonderfully connected in a world of disconnects is for you to know sure well how to successfully communicate. So, what is the essence of communication?

When two separate things communicate, they are working together to identify their purpose together. This is the first step of communication. It could be the remote control and the TV communicating, a car and a car key, a son and mother, a computer and the user, a cashier and the register, the judge and the defendant, the artist and the brush, or the paint and the canvas. Two things come together to participate together and thus they create something new.

The communication may be verbal, body language, silent, electronic, written, or actions. It is truly said that "actions speak louder than words." But what is the point of communication?

When your phone rings you may have no idea who is calling or why. Right away your instinct is to determine the purpose of the call. The same thing happens when we answer the front door, receive a piece of mail, or attend a meeting at work or school. Why are we here? What's the point?

We already know the general purpose of coming together in many circumstances, so there is normally some commonality for communication. We speak the same language, share many of the same circumstances, and we soon identify our common ground. This makes for easier communications.

A meeting at work usually has straightforward purposes, as does a classroom, but not so much with the family at home. One person came home from one job, one from school, etc. We have several different lives and experiences converging at once.

When family farms and family businesses were popular, the family worked together and had a great deal of common ground. The family dinner table used to be a popular meeting place. Even when holidays roll around, everybody knows to be as polite as possible to make the day go smoothly. But in the hectic days of today's bustling cities and towns, we have to make a concerted effort to lead our families toward healthy communications.

But communications are not always healthy and will not always help us connect with others. An alcoholic might tell his family he loves them more than anything and then miss an important family event because he can't stay sober. The family wants to believe his words but his actions speak volumes.

In turn, his wife may tell him she loves him dearly and then hold back her affection. The kids might similarly tell their parents how important the family is to them even as they stay as far away from home as they can.

The truth is that they are communicating two different things at once. That is called miscommunication. The person who miscommunicates is conflicted and may not even know it. When they say they are trying to save up money for a family vacation, they likely mean it. But then a great deal on a cell phone package or new clothes may entice them to reassess their priorities. They don't realize they have changed their priorities but instant gratification just won.

A way to avoid miscommunication is to be fully aware of what you are feeling and saying and to be very intentional in your communication. If you are just saying something to satisfy somebody and get them off your back, you are miscommunicating. If you are telling somebody what they want to hear but it is not what you want to say, you are miscommunicating. If you are deceitful or withholding pertinent information, you are miscommunicating. If you are using reverse psychology or some other tool of manipulation, you are miscommunicating. Even if you are living in silent rage, you are miscommunicating. Remember, communication is to send and receive accurate messages.

Although there are many ways to miscommunicate, there are as many ways to effectively communicate. Soft words communicate. Vocal inflection communicates. Gestures communicate. Slamming doors communicate. Fists in walls communicate. Sex communicates. Communication is made up of verbal and nonverbal communications. Even over the phone it is said that if you smile while you talk, the cheerfulness will be conveyed.

Communication through dark and difficult issues that are deeply interpersonal is no different. It is like navigating dangerous seas. The water may be murky and full of obstacles to navigate. There may be sea serpents lurking and fantasy islands beckoning. There may be driftwood from past shipwrecks and heavy kelp from past conversations slowing down the progress. These may hinder progress, but patience in communication will always prevail.

In turn, there may be many joyous things to be shared in the happy return of a sobering alcoholic to the fold. It may look like clear sailing until some storm clouds start to gather around the conversations. The point is this. We need to learn to facilitate effective communication because the communication process is our pathway to experiencing God, feeling connected to the people around us, and living in peace.

Good communication will empower old festering wounds to be opened as needed and the shrapnel removed and thrown away. The barbed words of the past can be retranslated into smoothed gestures of reconciliation and truth. Smiling lies and false pleasantries can be laid to rest as open hearts frankly and lovingly discuss their experiences without judging each other.

As we communicate and exchange emotional and intellectual intimacies with one another, we learn that all of us have handicaps within ourselves that can color our perceptions and cloud our judgment. Old thought processes can be recognized and set aside as needed. Emotions can be uncovered without feeling the need to justify our feelings. We learn that it is less important to be right in a conversation than it is to be fruitful in strengthening our family.

For many of us this new paradigm of communication sounds wonderful, but how do we do it? What barriers will we encounter? How long will it take?

The first thing we need to do is take a break and assess the situation. Are we convinced that we need to change or are we just looking for the other person to change? Are we able to admit our own faults and weaknesses or do we just want to point out those issues in others? Are we just seeking another quick fix? Will this new concept of communication be abused by us to control others, or will it lead to a fruitful way to build successes among us? Can it do any good if I learn to communicate but can't get any cooperation from others?

Some of these probing questions can be answered universally while other answers will be dependent upon the motives and abilities of others, as well as the circumstances and surroundings. Since we cannot speak for other people's motives, let's just be concerned about our own motives.

It may seem to some of us that we are flying solo on this mission, but we need to have confidence that God is always willing to be our pilot. Even though you are the only one who appears to be working on communication within your social circle, you can have confidence that change can and will happen if you commit yourself to the process.

Think of the missionaries of the bible. Think of Jesus. There were many people they communicated with that lived in darkness, but with the Father's guidance, their efforts to communicate the need for change were successful. Remember, God's word will not return void (Isaiah 55:11).

There are thousands of ways to miscommunicate but there are only a few rules to good communication. It will be important for you to know and practice good communication skills consistently until they become second nature.

First, prepare ahead of time. Pray alone before any important or difficult communication so that God is present and guiding as much of the process as people will allow. Your prayer for the situation will positively impact everybody involved and prepare your spirit to be aligned with God before you open your mouth. Conducting your affairs prayerfully and consistently may not seem like it is getting the immediate results you crave, but have confidence there will soon be dividends for your patience and humble prayers. If appropriate, as you start to meet, invite the others to pray with you if that is customary, but this can also create distance instead of closeness, so only invite others to pray at the beginning of the meeting if you know they will be comfortable with prayer. It is not a time to appear religious. Unwanted prayers may lend an impression that you are a religious bully or feel spiritually lofty.

Second, before the communication, identify the subject matter and posture of the communication. What exactly will be the topic discussed? Are you acting like a boss the boss or a subservient employee? Are you playing the role of parent or child? Are you perceived to be an enemy or a friend? Do you have an axe to grind and are you going in heavily armed and ready to fight?

In turn, do not pigeonhole anyone before the communication has a chance to reveal their interest. Maybe the prayer you said earlier for them will prepare them for healthy communication as well. Be prepared to stick to the topic so that extraneous issues don't detract from the subject at hand.

Third, remember that God has given us two ears and one mouth, mostly to be used in those proportions. Keep in mind that it is more important for you to understand than to be understood. Let's face it: you already know what you think. It is more important for you to know what they think. Of course, contrary to that are those people who think that others will benefit from what they think. Get over yourself!

People will want to benefit from what you think if you care about them, but people don't care how much you know until they know how much you care. Listening is a great way to show you care and establish rapport. Always take turns, and don't be afraid to also take your turn when it is time.

Fourth, good communication is a two-way street. The communication has to be received before it is complete. It is good if there is some confirmation or acknowledgment as to each talking point. It is also wise to conduct communications when the other party is free and able to concentrate on what is being said. Ask if it is a good time to talk. Otherwise you will not know if there has actually been a successful communication.

Fifth, be slow to judge and quick to admit your own weaknesses. It is vital that you confess your own weaknesses and hear and understand before you judge. James 5:16 tells us, "Confess your sins to each other and pray for each other so that you may be healed" (NLT).

Your confession will create an environment for healing and authenticity. Even if the other people aren't forthcoming with their own wrongs, don't judge them quickly. Remember, the judgment in a trial always comes after the talking points and arguments, never before. Also, a judgment has a chilling effect. It closes the two-way street.

Sixth, be brave and honest. It isn't communication if it is not honest. It's deception. It is okay to be persuasive, but not domineering or controlling. You are trying to understand each other and reach some common goals. That is the purpose of communication. You are not going to be able to create understanding by dancing around the truth.

Seventh, remain as calm as possible. A general rule of thumb is not to speak any louder than the other person as you make sure you state your case completely. Agitation doesn't facilitate communication in most cases. Signs of aggressiveness in conversation reduce the likelihood a common goal can be established or reached. If it gets loud or difficult, also give permission for it to get quiet and peaceful.

Finally, leave with things learned. At the end of a communication, there should be some newfound hope or knowledge, or perhaps a plan for improvement. If you can sum up the communication with "takeaway" points, that is good. The best case scenario would be for each person to be able to state what their "takeaways" are from each conversation they have. That often becomes your To Do list.

Also, keep in mind there are many communication opportunities that you can create. You can make plans for dinner at home or a picnic or outings at the park or lake. You might invite the family for a board game or home movie. Whatever the opportunity that will appeal to your people, keep in mind that you don't need to get results or need to feel like you have accomplished something in an attempt to establish a line of communication.

The fact that you have the family working together on something is itself communication. To press too much for "meaningful" communication is setting up the meeting to fail. Also, to setup the meeting with the expectation that there should be a certain quality of communication or certain outcome sets up failure. Be at peace in the process, take the right steps, and leave the results to God.

Our family is fully adjusted to having a "family meeting" as necessary, and it is always something positive. If your family meetings are not positive, they will be dreaded and avoided. It is best to offer three positive comments to one negative comment. Also, keep the well being of the family unit as the constant higher goal so that it doesn't become about trying to "fix" one person or accommodate one situation at the expense of others. Try to build consensus along the way and don't assume everybody is "on board."

In husband-wife communications, dinner out or bedroom romance can be helpful at times. Even a movie together at home after the children have gone to bed can be a victory moving toward communication.

Often times, romance is an embarrassing problem. Money is another frequent difficulty. The disobedience of young people can also present challenges in communication. The best time to discuss these things is not when things are difficult and people are on edge. When people are agitated they are more likely to argue to have their voice heard because they feel like their life is out of control. It is better to wait until things are calm, or at least civilized, to initiate communication.

Some people also make the mistake of thinking they can "set the tone" for successful communication. They might give the other partner what they enjoy, whether it be food, romance, favors or attention, and they might then bring up a difficult subject. The partner is then likely to feel like the goodwill created by the charitable act was faked in order to manipulate them into a conversation. Rather than manipulate a set of circumstances that will give you an opportunity to communicate, think of it differently. Just be willing to setup the favorable circumstances and see if the other person is willing to communicate.

Be led by God in your communication. Rule one was prayer. Perhaps your loved one will only seem to take advantage of your generosity at first, but might later come to trust you more because you are able to give without expectation of reciprocation. They might think well of your giving nature if it is consistent. So, always pray as you go about trying to create an environment that facilitates communication. Manifesting the presence of God in a quiet, cheerful way will never hurt the situation and it will create peace for you personally despite other difficulties.

Another helpful opportunity is to inquire about each person's day. Show interest in their concerns even if they seem small to you. This gives them a chance to express themselves in an open-ended discussion that may lead to fruitful talks. Also, they may well be intrigued by your genuine inquiry and start to reciprocate. Don't be surprised if they start asking about your day.

Some of us will be tempted to avoid communication entirely. We will go to great lengths to ignore the other person. It just seems we are not willing to go through the pain because we have so little hope for something good to come from it.

Most of us handle pain in one of two ways: either we are motivated into rash undertakings in order to rid ourselves of the pain, or we are paralyzed as we wait for the discomfort to pass on its own. In the midst of emotional pain and turmoil, we need to be able to identify our thoughts and feelings. Pain has a beginning, a middle, and an end. The hardest part is in the middle. For the duration of the middle of pain, we forget that there was a time when the pain did not exist, a beginning, and a time when the pain will not exist, an end.

The problem is not that we are in pain; the problem is that we lose hope in the middle of pain. To make matters worse, our culture reinforces the lie that something is wrong because we are experiencing pain. Why, we ask, would a God that is good allow me to experience pain?

It is simple. God uses pain to call our attention to the area of our life that needs some attention. Once we understand that pain is God's tool to reach out to us, we can see pain in a new light. God has a plan for our pain.

First, we need to know that pain is not forever. An old Hebrew proverb reads, "This too shall pass."

Second, we need to know that God does have a plan, despite any evidence that might seem to the contrary. Jeremiah 29:11 tells us, "For I know the plans I have for you," says the LORD. "They are plans for good and not for disaster, to give you a future and a hope" (NLT).

Third, we need to know that the high cost of our pain is God's way of making sure that we treasure the lesson we learn. Thomas Paine wisely penned, "What we obtain too cheap, we esteem too lightly."

While we may never get to the point where we embrace emotional pain, while we may only grudgingly endure our painful lessons, if we can recall that pain is a teacher sent from God, we might be more willing to proceed on a sane course of communications that leads to peace. The pain always begins to lessen as we find peace.

While we struggle under the duress of emotional pain, waiting for peace and understanding to heal us, we should make no major decisions. We are otherwise likely to say things or take actions that will increase our pain and lengthen the healing process. Indeed, many actions may never be undone.

While distraught, we should attempt to find the neutral path that exist between rash actions and fearful paralysis. This means we should only be doing what we would normally do, regardless of the pain we're experiencing.

Maintaining a mundane routine during these times can be beneficial. On particularly difficult days it can be helpful to engage in menial busy tasks. If you are numb and dazed, it is important not to engage in activities that might present a hazard to you or others.

Farris is fond of remembering two things when he feels like he is in trouble, and jokingly says he has two brain cells left to safeguard those two ideals. One brain cell is named Humility and his twin is named Service. Like twins, they need each other, often times desperately so. So, when Farris falters, he needs to find something to do where he can be humble and also be of service. He often shares that when things are really going bad he likes to wash the family dishes by hand because it is something constructive he can do for others without doing any further damage or endangering himself. Our family is happy to report that, so far, not a dish has been broken!

While in this process of waiting for our pain to subside, we should pray and meditate more, and read more, increasing our dependence upon God. Only He can guide us through the worst of the middle of pain just as He guides us through the valley of the shadow of death (Psalm 23:4).

Ronald Reagan said, "Peace is not the absence of conflict; it is the ability to handle conflict by peaceful means." Conflict is intentional by God's design. Conflict, like pain, is our teacher.

If we are not careful, we misunderstand the seventh Beatitude about being peacemakers, thinking that we must make peace by avoiding conflict. On the contrary, our personal resources don't contain peace; it's God's peace, not ours (John 14:27).

We should forget about trying to feel peaceful. We should forget about trying to make peace. Neither should we intentionally create discord, since conflict will occur on God's schedule, not ours. Instead, we should borrow God's peace, planting it firmly in our hearts, and enter into conflict and communications prepared for spiritual growth.

"SERENITY, CALMNESS, PEACE, NIRVANA, ENLIGHTENMENT.... I JUST CAN'T TAKE THE **PRESSURE** ANY MORE!"

The Wisdom of Solomon

One day King Solomon decided to humble his most trusted minister. He said to him, "Benaiah, there is a certain ring that I want you to bring to me. I wish to wear it for Sukkot. That gives you six months to find it."

"If it exists anywhere on earth, your majesty," replied Benaiah, "I will find it and bring it to you, but what makes the ring so special?" "It has magic powers," answered Solomon. "If a happy man looks at it, he becomes sad, and if a sad man looks at it, he becomes happy." Solomon knew that no such ring existed in the world, but he wished to give his minister a little taste of humility for Sukkot, the holiday that reminds the Israelites of their difficult exodus out of Egypt.

Spring and summer passed, and still Benaiah had no idea where he could find the ring. On the eve of Sukkot, he decided to take a walk in a poor area of Jerusalem. He passed by a merchant who had begun to set out the day's wares on a shabby rug. "Have you by any chance heard of a magic ring that makes the happy wearer forget his joy and the broken-hearted wearer forget his sorrows?" asked Benaiah.

He watched the old man take a plain gold ring from his carpet and engrave something on it. When Benaiah read the words on the ring, his face broke out in a wide smile.

That night the entire city welcomed in the holiday of Sukkot with great festivity. "Well, my friend," said Solomon, "have you found what I sent you after?" All the ministers laughed and Solomon himself smiled.

To everyone's surprise, Benaiah held up a small gold ring and declared, "Here it is, your majesty!" As soon as Solomon read the inscription, the smile vanished from his face. The jeweler had written three Hebrew letters on the gold band: "gimel, zayin, yud," which began the words "Gam zeh ya'avor" -- "This too shall pass."

At that moment Solomon realized that all his wisdom and fabulous wealth and tremendous power were but fleeting things, for one day he would be nothing but dust.

Recovery Models

There are two general schools of thought regarding recovery from alcoholism even though there are also different types of treatment. A careful examination of the different types of treatment will be the subject of another book because the subject is complex and deserves an exhaustive discussion. Let it suffice now to present the central point to be made about different treatment types. Simply put, people respond differently to different treatment types, and that response also varies at different times in the life of the subject.

Meanwhile, the polarization of general philosophies regarding recovery boils down to two different models as to what constitutes legitimate long-term recovery. One is the Deliverance Model and the other is the Process Model. Both of these models typically use education and treatment as part of their approach because knowing the dangers of alcoholism helps create motivation for either model.

In addition to the two basic models, there are different systems of care within each model. Alcoholics Anonymous (A.A.) is the original 12-step program and spawned Al-Anon Family Groups as well as, in recent years, some 12-step based Christian ministries. The arena for Christian ministries are churches that are friendly toward people seeking recovrery, but not all Christian ministries are 12-step based or conscious of the needs of the family.

There are often highly charged emotions and entrenched thoughts regarding this subject matter. Some readers may have strong beliefs that will prevent them from keeping an open mind. Thus, we want to ensure the reader now that God approves of sobriety (Ephesians 5:18), perceives drunkenness as sin (Galatians 5:21), and also wants us to continue to humbly work out our deliverance (Philippians 2:12).

Conservative Christians often favor the Deliverance Model more. Generally, they believe that God has delivered the alcoholic from their alcoholism, that the alcoholic needs to turn away from their past and live in the newly found freedom they have been granted. Adherents to this model are more likely to perceive alcoholism as sin and usually do not believe that a person is "born alcoholic." They are also more likely to appreciate abstinence as evidence of change.

The loved ones of alcoholics often "buy into" the Deliverance Model also when they think that the alcoholic being sober solves their problems, that somehow they too have been delivered. The transference of the blessing of sobriety from the alcoholic to the nonalcoholic loved one is a strong lure, but it removes the responsibility the nonalcoholic has for maintaining sanity. For them, in this model, they are still living off of the alcoholic's sobriety instead of being primarily concerned with their own emotional sanity. That is pure proof that they are codependent and need help.

Adherents to the Deliverance Model are more likely to object to Alcoholics Anonymous (A.A.) participation. They don't think of "recovery" as the goal. They want the alcoholic to consider themselves as "recovered" and don't like the idea of them continuing to attend meetings in which they might continue to identify themselves as an "alcoholic" in recovery. They may believe that people who self-identify as an alcoholics are affirming their alcoholism when they should be denying it.

A rigidly religious deliverance model is also likely to say that you cannot be a Christian and an alcoholic. That philosophy, simply put, believes the two are mutually exclusive. They might also have trouble reconciling the claims of the Apostle Paul that he still sinned after he was saved. In any event, it is naïve to think Christians no longer sin after salvation.

If you will recall the story of Dalton and Fran, they attended church and Dalton went to the altar with some frequency, praying to be delivered, receiving some relief, only to return to his alcoholic drinking within months. Within the Deliverance Model of treatment, it is acceptable to go to the altar but the goal must be to fully repent and never return to drink. Anybody who thinks deliverance will supply an alcoholic with the ability to control their drinking is delusional and likely to live a life full of nightmarish struggles.

Going to the altar is a great idea as a one-day experience of repentance, but the success of an alcoholic is going to be more dependent upon them being willing to *live at the altar*, to be bowed down before God daily in their heart. Those who have been delivered and gone back and forth may eventually find that God takes His hand off of them and allows them to wallow in their sordid self indulgence for the rest of their life. We have seen such sad cases too many times.

Alcoholic families often think it is unfair of God to allow some people to drink successfully and others to drown in alcoholic nightmares. They believe that God is good and couldn't abandon their loved one.

What they don't see is that God never abandons His children, but that He may quit bailing them out of trouble. That is what the entire family needs to learn to do.

Alcoholism is no longer a curse to our own family. Now it has become a blessing. It has empowered us to avoid selfish indulgences and has instead provided us a mission in life. God has used our affliction to teach us and give us direction, but only after we made peace with God.

Indeed, many of humanity's difficulties in life are allowed by God to exist so that we learn humility and service. These difficulties only seem to be a curse because we are busy trying to manage our lives instead of allowing God to work through us. In short, our own inherited fleshly curses are used by God to call us to partake in the joy and relief of His blessing.

This can be astonishingly difficult for the alcoholic family to understand. Everybody is struggling to control something and God lives silently in the background. The alcoholic is focused on alcohol. The family is focused on the alcoholic. Nobody is focused on God. Each soul has only focused on the results they seek.

At some point, the alcoholic may well question his salvation. The family might also wonder. Their pastor may want to add an opinion to the mix. Friends might also suggest things. They all may wonder if the alcoholic is really a Christian.

People are never going to be able to answer these questions. The answers belong to God as does the judgment of each person's salvation. Let it suffice to say that the deliverance model should not entice people to condemn and accuse each other of not belonging to God. It should rather highlight the need for an absolute repentance followed up by perfect abstinence and a daily devout program of spiritual growth and selfless service. Leave the theological discussions alone as you work to save the alcoholic and the family.

Meanwhile, the Process Model of recovery focuses on the path of recovery without being as concerned about the destination. They believe the process involves ongoing effort and that an alcoholic is always in recovery and will remain in process until they draw their last sober breath.

This applies to the family as well as the alcoholic. For the families, their sanity, as opposed to sobriety, is an ongoing work that is not dependent upon the alcoholic's sobriety. They too will have to engage in a lifelong process in order to maintain that sanity.

This Process Model is more likely founded in 12-step organizations, treatment centers, and within many Christian spiritual environments that realize sympathetically how difficult it is for an alcoholic to recover from alcoholism. Success in a process model environment is based upon a steady effort resulting in progress over time.

Both models are successful but incomplete without each other. If a person engages in a process of spiritual development without a spiritual awakening having occurred, they will lose the heart to continue on this difficult path. In turn, if an alcoholic is dramatically delivered but doesn't engage in a healthy spiritual process of abstinence, self-confrontation and growth, they will likely try sometime to exhibit their victory over substance abuse by partaking in moderation. We have known alcoholics and families that think the use of alcohol in moderation is the sign that somebody has been delivered.

This is similar to the snake-handling believers that engage in serpent handling rituals. If they are perfectly in the Spirit of God, no worldly thing can destroy them (Mark 16:17-18 and Luke 10:19). Unfortunately, many Christians feel the need to prove they are invincible and many of the snake handling believers have been killed or maimed. Similarly, an alcoholic engages in the same type of vanity when they try to prove they can control their intake of alcohol. They want to prove they are cured because they are not satisfied with the simple solution of living a sober life.

Jesus was quite clear that if your hand or eye offends you, pluck it out (Matthew 5:29 and Mark 9:43). Since the mind of the alcoholic cannot be plucked out, instead we must learn to take alcoholic thoughts captive (2 Corinthians 10:5). Progress occurs as the mind continues to be conformed to Christ (John 3:30 and Romans 12:2). Any return to alcohol after your house has been swept clean (Matthew 12:43-45), but left without the daily filling of the Spirit of God (Ephesians 5:18), invites still worst disaster. We are not to only obey when we feel like it. People who have been delivered have a mandate to honor that deliverance...it is their cross to bear (Luke 9:23). Our very own family has a blessing that has come from a curse, but we are not cured. We are delivered each day as we honor Jesus (Romans 8:12-17).

The family may also feel, at times, that the alcoholic is cured. The family may start to make hasty and hopeful decisions based upon that wishful thinking. To complicate things, the family may not sense a need for change in their own lives. In these cases, the alcoholic may have been delivered but is still living with a family that has not sensed any additional need for change. The family's perception that all is well once the alcoholic is sober doesn't empower the family to support sobriety. They don't see any need for them to change and will likely continue some of their own enabling behaviors without realizing it. They are happy just to live peacefully in the alcoholic's deliverance.

While deliverance is certainly essential, it is not deliverance if it doesn't stay delivered. That is where we again pick up with the Process Model.

Whether the alcoholic has had a dramatic spiritual experience, or just desires a change, it is essential they take this deliverance to the next level of commitment, a desire for a lifetime of sobriety. For the family, they normally experience the same dramatic change because they feel delivered from the havoc and danger alcoholism has brought to their home, and they too must commit to actively maintaining a spirit of sanity in the home. While the alcoholic is at the beginning of staying physically sober, the family is now at the beginning of staying emotionally sober.

The problem with that concept is that nobody can stay sober, or sane, forever. One can only stay sober here and now.
The old phrase, One Day at a Time, may be overused and trivialized, but is as true as it ever was. Yesterday's sobriety was terrific but doesn't mean much if I am not in the process of staying sober today. Tomorrow's sobriety is never quite certain, so today is the only day the Lord has made for us to be sober.

While the thought of living one day at a time may comfort those who can live with fluidity in their life, it troubles people who would like to think they can make a sober commitment and never again fail. In turn, people who are only staying sober for today may have no deep inner desire or commitment for a lifetime of sobriety. Either person can fail.

The truth is that both models make for a perfect and complete method. We receive a reprieve from alcoholism when we repent and follow up gratefully each day by choosing sobriety day after day. Farris recently celebrated ten thousand days sober, twice the length of time he dwelled in the hellish depths of alcoholism.

It works to have a daily process, but only if there has been a life choice to stay sober. Think of what the Apostle Paul meant when he instructed the faithful in Philippians 2:12 to "...continue to work out your salvation with fear and trembling" (NIV). The act of working out alcoholic redemption is a daily process filled with humility and sustained effort.

Some thirty years ago, when Farris was in a brief 2-year period of sobriety while still in his twenties, he reasoned that God would not want him to go through the rest of his life with the alcoholic label on his forehead. He soon quit attending meetings with other alcoholics. Six months later he thought it would be okay to display the power of God by showing he had power over alcohol. He began to drink again at age 29 and almost never came out of it.

By the grace of God, there was yet another moment of clarity that was made available for Farris at age 31, but only after many months of increasing difficulties and personal losses. God did not make it easy for Farris to get sober that last time, nor did God make it easy for Farris to stay sober.

In his previous periods of sobriety, Farris was able to glide on the pink cloud of sobriety and stay sober while not enduring much difficulty with the process. The problem was that Farris did not have an appreciation of how precious a gift he had been given. He took it for granted, thought he could still somehow control it, and set out to prove he was not powerless over alcohol. His goal was to show he had dominion over alcohol. His mistake was that he thought he had to show his power over alcohol by taking it into his system, instead of being at peace simply resisting the temptation.

The folly of such logic is common. Think of Christ being tempted in the desert. Did Jesus need to show His power over the devil by partaking of the devil's temptation? Certainly not. Jesus showed us how to resist the devil, not appease him. In turn, alcoholics must resist temptation, not try to control it or cave into it. For the alcoholic, the only victory over alcohol is the victory that empowers us not to partake.

The philosophical conflict between the 12-step approach and some Christian beliefs has been going on for decades. We would like to settle those accounts for the reader here and now. It is of no spiritual profit to subscribe to one or the other. We strongly suggest that you not allow the prideful prejudice of closed minds within either camp prevent you from finding the Great Hope of Christ at every turn.

Regarding 12-step groups like Alcoholics Anonymous, let's consider the word of God. A complaint among some Christians is that A.A. is idol worship because A.A. allows for people to pick a god of their own understanding. Regarding that "higher power" concept, Paul had an interesting experience in Athens.

In the book of Acts we find that Paul was also troubled by idols and he used the nondescript gods to lead nonbelievers to Jesus. Finally Paul was brought before the philosophical leaders of Athens and spoke about the unknown God: "He is the God who made the world and everything in it. Since he is Lord of heaven and earth, he doesn't live in manmade temples...His purpose in all of this was that the nations should seek after God and perhaps feel their way toward him and find him--though he is not far from any one of us...God overlooked people's former ignorance about these things, but now he commands everyone everywhere to turn away from idols and turn to him" (Acts 17:16-30 NLT).

A.A.'s spiritual program may not be the pure form of worship we like to think we enjoy, but A.A. provides sobriety so that alcoholics may "feel their way toward him and find him." Truly, that is not unlike the way God works in the background for every pre-Christian. He is constantly bringing forth the circumstances that will humble us before Him and lead us into repentance, and alcoholism is clearly a humbling foe.

The A.A. program came out of a movement of faithful follow-ers of Christ known as the Oxford Group. Their name prior to 1928 had been "A First Century Christian Fellowship." In 1931, in England, a London newspaper reporter, A.J. Russell, attended an Oxford Group meeting with the intention of exposing the group. He wrote, "I came as an observer and became a convert!"

In 1932 and 1933, a former Rhode Island State Senator who was the son of wealthy mill owners, had become a hopeless alcoholic. In his quest for help he sought out the world famous psychiatrist, Sig-mund Freud, but Freud was too busy to see him. Some psychiatric experts now maintain that was a great blessing. The man instead consulted with the also famous Dr. Carl Jung, an advocate of spiritual experiences. It is thought that Freud would have surely mocked this man's later spiritual conversion as neurotic.

Jung told him there was no hope for him there in his office, and to go home and possibly find a conversion through some religious group. The man joined up with the Oxford Group in the United States and be-came sober. They taught him certain principles that he applied to his life. The principles taught were later spelled out in a story told by one of A.A.'s founders, Bill Wilson:

> We admitted we were licked.
> We got honest with ourselves.
> We talked it over with another person.
> We made amends to those we had harmed.
> We tried to carry this message to others with no thought of re-ward.
> We prayed to whatever god we thought there was.

Is there something ungodly in this? We think not. Rather, if mature Christians eat the meat of the Word of God, and new Christians live on the milk of the Word, then certainly alcoholics and pre-Christians could live on the colostrum-like pre-milk of A.A.

For those of you unaware, colostrum is the first milk from a moth-er that prepares the infant for life, offering immunities to disease and providing body building proteins. What an appropriate concept for al-coholics—they get their first taste of life from other alcoholics who have found God in recovery, and even though they are not ready to believe and understand, they are at least now sober and able to walk the path.

To address another concern, there is no idol worship in A.A. There is only a beginning to find God that begins with sobriety. Certainly Satan doesn't want these drunks getting sober. What gain could there be in him releasing those enslaved? It would be a great stretch to say that Satan is sobering them up so that they can worship a godless idol. Indeed, the many people who find Christ because of their sobriety are staggering in comparison! So, how can we denounce sobriety in A.A. without denouncing every non-Christian hospital and doctor on the planet?

To be fair, and to leave no stone unturned, we have also seen a prejudice against religion by some of the people in 12-step groups. Some 12-steppers think of themselves as more spiritual than those of us who are religious. Sometimes, 12-step people are willing to call religious people hypocrites because religious people can be judgmental and still commit sins in their lives.

The real hypocrisy here is that 12-steppers can choose to be hard on Christians even as they largely overlook the sin and character defects among other 12-step members. They are more forgiving of alcoholics or addicts because "at least they are trying to stay sober," inferring that religious people are not trying to stay free of sin. Using the low threshold of sobriety, many 12-step people consider a success anybody who simply stays sober without accountability for other sinful behavior.

It is also hypocritical for 12-steppers to sit in a church to have their meeting and brag how they are more spiritual than the religious people who built the church where they meet. Still, society mostly thanks God, even for the ungrateful 12-steppers who are sober. People seem to know that recovering alcoholics are not going to get well right away.

Besides, throughout life, there is plenty of hypocrisy to go around. Opinions abound, but what does God say? Simply said, pride and claims of superiority are as filthy rags to God (Isaiah 64:6). As we go forth in life, we should all spend less time pointing fingers and more time reaching out with hands.

Folks, if you're concerned about all of the hypocrites in church, don't worry... We've room for one more.

What Causes Alcoholism?

Children of alcoholics are four times more likely to become alcoholics, according to the American Academy of Child & Adolescent Psychiatry, but they caution that environmental factors could also be at play.

Meanwhile, a Swedish study tracked alcohol use in twins who were adopted out as children and to different adoptive families. The occurrence of alcoholism was slightly higher among people who were exposed to alcoholism only through their adoptive families, thus showing a minor increase in alcoholism from environmental or behavioral factors. However, it was dramatically higher among the twins whose biological fathers were alcoholics, regardless of the presence of alcoholism in their adoptive families.

So, while people may have a genetic tendency to develop alcoholism, it does not guarantee they will become an alcoholic, but they are clearly at higher risk. Then what is the difference between an alcoholic and non-alcoholic? Is it genetic?

In Numbers 14:18 we read, "The LORD is slow to anger and filled with unfailing love, forgiving every kind of sin and rebellion. But he does not excuse the guilty. He lays the sins of the parents upon their children; the entire family is affected--even children in the third and fourth generations." (NLT) This would seem to indicate that the alcoholism of our ancestors is somehow visited upon the current generation. Does that mean that if my father were an alcoholic that I am doomed?

Then in Deuteronomy 24:16 we read, ""Parents must not be put to death for the sins of their children, nor children for the sins of their parents. Those deserving to die must be put to death for their own crimes" (NLT). That seems to say that I am not doomed even though my father may have chosen alcoholic self-destruction.

To complicate matters still more, we have studies that clearly cite evidence for the genetic inheritance of alcoholism as well as suggesting that family behavior and environment are strong contributing factors. So how can we sort through all of this?

Genetics is a relatively new science for mankind, but who invented genetics? Certainly not the scientists who started to uncover the human genome in 1988, nor the theorists of the last hundred and fifty years. Is it possible that God created genetics as His way of infusing His spiritual laws into the human condition? Could that help us to understand why we are able to be so smart and invent so many things and still be so ignorant about the mysteries of the human psyche?

If so, we would expect to see an increased incidence of alcoholism within the offspring of alcoholics' ancestors. Well, it is true that we see an increased amount of alcoholism, but nowhere near 100% of offspring from alcoholic ancestors become alcoholics. How do we reconcile this with scripture?

I have heard bible expositors mistakenly say that God's promise to pass along the iniquity of the fathers is no longer in play. They say that one is only responsible for one's own sin. They cite the verse from Deuteronomy 24:16. Here is the truth. They are half right.

According to Deuteronomy 24:16, we only suffer for our own sin. An expositor is correct to say that a person is not doomed to alcoholism, but they are not correct to say they are not cursed with the genetic predisposition. The iniquity of the father is visited upon the children but they are not doomed to commit the same sin. So, how does this play out in a person's life? Nobody is born an alcoholic even thought they might be born with a predisposition that makes them react differently to alcohol as it enters their system.

We will use Farris as an example. He knows that there has been alcoholism in his family history. He didn't know that when he was growing up and he didn't perceive any alcohol abuse in his home. Still, alcohol was not forbidden and some non-blood relatives drank normally and didn't seem to get in trouble.

Farris thought that alcohol was a life enhancing rite of passage into manhood and had his first drink when he was 13 years old. He was with other young friends at the time and drank a relatively small amount, but it immediately affected him. What Farris experienced then and thereafter was a comforting feeling from drinking. It put him at ease. Eventually he wreaked despair from his drinking, but he wouldn't have been as likely to begin a life of alcoholic self indulgence if he didn't have the genetic appetite toward the feeling created by alcohol consumption.

Remember the normal drinker who has half a glass of wine, pushes it away, and says, "I've had enough." That person did not receive the genetic inheritance that Farris did, and that is why Farris had to give up alcohol intake once and for all. Alternatively, as mentioned earlier, he could have stubbornly tried to control his drinking, lived a more miserable existence and died in the process, taking much of his family with him.

Because of our personal family experience, we have taught our sons to beware of alcohol and informed them that they will probably find it easy to become addicted to it. We have strongly suggested that they not drink at all ever, just because of Farris and his family.

Does that seem unfair? Is it cheating our sons out of the possibility of a pleasant experience? One might argue that perhaps they escaped this genetic inheritance. But what if they have not?

It would not be fair for us to allow them to die a thousand deaths by living an alcoholic life even for a short time. The potential for damages outweighs the likelihood of benefit. Consider what in life necessitates a drink. Farris has attended many events and marriages without drinking, even our own marriage. Cocktail parties are not a problem for us, and Ruth helps make for merriment without partaking as well. Nobody cares if we drink or not, so why should we? Truly, people usually only care if they feel they need something to feel better about themselves.

We are not against alcohol, but we don't endorse its use. Thousands of years ago, before such a high percentage of the population fell prey to alcoholism, before entire families dwelled in their selfish addictions, it might have been okay to drink. The bible indicates moderation.

So, we agree that it is okay to drink in moderation and we also suggest that you needn't indulge, even if you are not an alcoholic. At this point in mankind's existence, it is probably wise for mankind to find better alternatives for our culture. Also, many spiritual people agree that we might be creating a stumbling block for others by showing unspoken approval of liquor consumption (Romans 14:13). In any event, our family wouldn't want our drinking to encourage the wrong person to think they should also be able to drink.

There is a slogan among alcoholics in recovery: "There's nothing going so bad in life that a drink can't make it worse." At the very least, when a person does drink and encounters any difficulty whatsoever, whether they attribute it to the drinking or not, we can count on the fact that drinking doesn't make any situation any better. The only advantage a drink brings to the table is a comforting, and we can unequivocally state that seeking our comfort from the Spirit of God is always the preferred method.

But many pre-alcoholics will ignore the early warning signs of alcoholism and a new path unfolds. Once the temptation has its way with us, it is too late. An alcoholic who drinks initially denies it is a problem, and that denial entrenches the drinker. They refuse to see it as a problem because it has become their solution. The people around them can soon see it, but the drinker just thinks they are worrisome, that is, until the alcoholic almost destroys their life and becomes a slave to it.

Another contributing factor to alcoholism is peer pressure and environment. We have known people to become alcoholics even though they hated the taste and didn't like the effect it had on them, at least at first. Alcohol became an acquired taste for them.

They drink because it helps them fit into their social circle, whether it is the guys from work, a nightclub, an artist enclave, a soccer team, or some friends from school. The alcoholic in such groups encourages the pre-alcoholics to "have fun" by drinking and loosening up. Even though the pre-alcoholic may just drink sociably for months, there is eventually a "tipping point" where emotional strain from other environmental issues makes the effect of alcohol more desirable. It may be precipitated by a broken relationship, a lost job, or financial problems. Once a pre-alcoholic is socializing in an environment where alcohol has been identified as a sure way to relieve stress, a pre-alcoholic can take their temporary misfortune and turn it into a permanent tragedy, just by letting the bottle provide them relief from the misfortune.

These drinkers that have become alcoholics are not easily lost in the bottle. They don't have the genetic predisposition to immediately fall in love with the booze. They might also recover quickly if there are some serious adverse circumstances that result from getting drunk. They may have an arrest, lose a job, crash a car, make a scene somewhere, or even destroy a good relationship. Still, the consequences of drinking are not what will identify them as alcoholics. Their inability to quit drinking when they realize they should quit is what will clearly point to alcoholism. The drinkers who are attracted to social circle drinking will usually be able to quit unless they have the genetic predisposition. Despite any adversity, real alcoholics will continue to drink even though they may blame it on their social circle.

Meanwhile, the pre-alcoholic drinker is at a breaking point. Are they to be the beginning of a new and horrible legacy that might well be passed along to their descendants? Those pre-alcoholics who don't quit when they start to experience consequences will many times power through their concerns about alcoholism. They either want so desperately to be part of the social circle or they just need to change the way they feel.

Perhaps they grew up where feelings were stuffed and not discussed. Perhaps they don't know another way to deal with their difficulties and just want a little bit of comfort. Drinking may be the easiest way for them to avoid confrontation, isolation, or even the desperation of suicidal thinking. It is like medicine that helps them cope.

Farris has dealt with many men who grew up in good homes with sober parents and with no known alcoholic ancestors. In such cases, there is usually a variety of human characteristics and social/family influences that lead the man to seek some alternatives to the impossibly perfect family. When a child is young and feeling awkward, they may not have a safe way to learn about the feelings of maturing teens.

A young person usually grows up feeling like they must be a "Good Child." Once they start to experience the desires of the flesh, the child will likely become emotionally conflicted between their public image of Good Child and their increasingly provocative natural urges. The child may start with some behavior that the family mistakenly criticizes. This criticism will push the child toward secrecy in their chosen behaviors.

It would be better to first discuss behaviors and assess the situation and pray for how to handle it. The behavior could be relatively harmless behavior regarding food, reading books, listening to music, watching TV, playing sports, or fashion fads. It could be more serious issues like hanging out with shady friends, riding skateboards all over town, staying out at night, sexual exploration, or alcohol and drugs.

Once the child's behavior has been discussed, not criticized, the child's behavior should be monitored. The family must engage in helpful communications at these critical stages. It is important to build consensus with the child and give them healthy alternatives to their unacceptable behavior.

In any event, the family environment can heap coals of guilt upon an otherwise obedient child if they are not careful. A parent who fails to knock when they enter the youth's bedroom is asking for trouble. If the child is indulging themselves privately and feels violated, the parent has compromised the child's self-image and "outed" them without permission or emotional preparation. Bursts of distrust and anger are likely to follow. In turn, a parent should not hesitate to enter a room a few moments after knocking, always apologizing for the interruption and stating their cause.

If the parent shows distrust of the child, the child will also no longer trust that the parent is able to understand. A rude parent will have already shown their lack of respect for a child's boundaries and it will be much more difficult to parent the child on sensitive subjects. A humiliated child is likely to delve deeper into any secrets thoughts or diversions and feel ever more distant from the parent.

Many parents might argue that they have a right to know all about their children's behavior. This might be legally true but it doesn't build trust into the relationship. If a child's self-image suffers, they have few avenues for redemption. If they are "caught" doing something sinful or unhealthy, the humiliation they suffer drives them deeper still into shame and secrecy. At this point, some parents become more demanding and militant rather than conciliatory.

It would be wise for a parent to apologize profusely to their child for any unwelcome intrusions into the child's life. Once the immediate emotional trauma subsides, then the parent might be in a position to sit quietly with the child and discuss the traumatic series of events. If so, the child may grow healthy and build a new, more mature self-image. If not, distrust will likely grow and fuel a greater chasm between the parent and child, almost certainly leading to further difficulties.

The damage done by otherwise good homes is done unknowingly. That is why family communication is essential. Our children must have confidence in which they are becoming. If they don't feel good about themselves, they will find something to make them feel good, and drugs or alcohol may find a way into their life.

There are so many nuances to healthy communication, family awareness, good parenting, and discipline, we recommend that the children be part of family decision making as early as possible so that they can rightfully include the family as their primary peer group. Still, you don't have to be their buddy or let them run the family; you simply make an effort to include them along the way so they know they are an important part of a healthy family.

We also recommend that families study parenting books that focus on both love and discipline. Both are essential. Heaping amounts of love without discipline feels like permissiveness to the child and they grow up without healthy human boundaries. They think they are supposed to do what they want.

Heaping amounts of discipline without love feels like punishment and the child has difficulty with God and love for the rest of their life. They then feel they can't do anything right.

Just like God loves and disciplines us, this is the model for how we share our love and discipline. We first show love for ourselves and exhibit healthy disciplines in our own life and with our spouse. It is then easier to share that with our children as they grow.

As members of our family grow into being the persons that God created, try to honor the sovereign nature of each soul. You are the parent for a time, but God is the Creator. Our role as parents is to give our children roots from which to grow and wings with which to soar. This will best prepare them to stand firmly in Christ.

Evil is Real

As we move forward in understanding alcoholism, it is important to know there is a spiritual battle taking place within the life of every alcoholic, and usually throughout the family as well. If we are to believe what God says and put stock in spiritual realities, we realize as spiritual beings having a human experience that there are also spiritual beings not having a human experience. Those are angels.

Many people like to think of angels that help us but refuse to consider there may be demons that work against us. Rather than convince you, I would suggest that you keep an open mind on the subject. If there is good, there is evil. If there is no evil, then it's all good.

The bible clearly discusses good and evil. We don't like to focus on evil, but we know it exists. The focus for us will be to discuss what evil has to do with alcoholism and recovery.

You will recall that alcohol is also referred to as spirits. Does that mean that we become more susceptible to spiritual influences when we drink? It is interesting that the Greek word for pharmacy has the same meaning as sorcery. God knew we were playing with fire when we went past drinking in moderation and got drunk, eventually choosing to ingest a variety of poisons for the temporary pleasure these drugs provide.

To what extent we subject ourselves to evil depends largely on how deeply dependent we become on alternative realities. If we cannot reconcile ourselves with our lives as they are, we try to find alternatives. This is when we become susceptible to evil.

God would like for us to stay on the straight and narrow. He will even give loud and clear signals when we stray, but He will not keep us from evil if we pursue it time and again. Our mistake is that we misinterpret reality and think the "feel good" experiences we have are heading in the right direction.

How can something that feels so good be wrong? Many a ballad has been written about the forbidden delicacies of life. We indulge ourselves as we glorify our excitement and ignore the dangers. God calls it sin when we put our feelings ahead of His laws, and that has been our fleshly quest since Eden. It is an easy pitfall to find.

At first, an alcoholic may get drunk and suffer only minor consequences. He might think, "This is great! I'm bulletproof!" God and His angels might keep that same alcoholic alive through some other difficult times. But the alcoholic might well continue to ignore God and drink to oblivion.

The sad truth is that God is trying to reach the alcoholic the entire time, but the alcoholic focuses on the apparent benefit of alcohol rather than notice the signals that something is wrong in his life. It is like a driver ignoring road signs and traffic signals, driving without any sense of reality. His family is sitting beside him or in the back seat, praying for safety, increasingly vocalizing their concerns as they sit helpless and powerless to do anything. They may even try to take over the wheel at times, only to see a violent battle ensue for control.

In the alcoholic's life initially, a boss or a family member might say something about his drinking problem and the alcoholic might blow right through that "Dangerous Curves Ahead" sign offered by God. Then he might be fired from work, and instead of seeing his drinking as a contributing factor, he might blame his boss, refusing to hesitate for serious reflection at God's stop sign. He continues drinking, wanting and trying to feel better about himself, even as alcohol becomes his constant companion and primary life solution. He isolates from people and lives increasingly in solitary delusion. Soon he is running God's red lights with reckless abandon. Before long, he is racked up in a hospital bed and God finally has his undivided attention.

The alcoholic may get out of the hospital and stay sober for a while, but he is now handicapped. The damage has already been done. His brain has been trained to appreciate the influence of alcohol and he has become accustomed to the little voice in his head that helps him to justify his drinking.

A temporarily sober alcoholic that has just experienced sufficient consequences to get his attention is usually not done drinking. He is taking a break and recuperating, building favor with the family and world, even while his alcoholic mind continues to stalk him. He may even say he is repulsed by alcohol as he battles daily against the temptation within him.

He doesn't share these persistent thoughts about drinking because it is embarrassing. He doesn't want to appear weak and unable to control his own life so he pretends, even convincing himself, that he can manage to resist temptation. If he doesn't get help, he is almost certainly doomed. Alone with the persistent nagging desire to drink, he will eventually falter. He might devise a way to secretly drink, or proudly announce that he can now control his drinking, but he will find some way to drink if he cannot quiet his alcoholic mind. He doesn't see any evil in these mental processes, nor will the family. We all want to believe our thoughts are exclusively under our control.

When the alcoholic turns himself over to the spirits in the bottle, he not only loses control for the moment, but he also lessens his ability to resist future temptations. He may well continue to belong to God, but the mind has begun to be permanently affected. He has, in reality, lost partial control of his faculties.

Farris works daily with alcoholics and addicts who have lost their way with God. Some of them have become unable to distinguish their "real" self from the delusional mind they work with each day. Many of them have never had a sufficient relationship with God to even know what to expect from a healthy mind. With prolonged substance usage, they become lost in their fantastic notions and spiral out of control, grasping at straws around them like a drowning man, hoping to find a successful set of circumstances and a stable reality where they can comfortably dwell.

Their family witnesses their slow decay and fails to realize the person has lost control of their life. The alcoholic can usually still carry on a conversation, show up to work, eat and get dressed, but not always. In any event, the outward appearance of the alcoholic scarcely reflects the oppression within their mind.

Farris reached the depths of his demoralization at a time in life when he was working, living in a nice neighborhood, and driving a brand new car. He had quit going to church many years earlier, but he still considered himself a Christian who loved Jesus. The problem was that he couldn't face life without the assistance of booze and drugs. He had become dependent upon the substance instead of God. This is the bottom line for every soul. We cannot replace God in our lives with anything.

We know that sobriety is what an alcoholic must have first, before anything. The booze and drugs have created an opening for evil to attack and disable them. Even though the person may belong to God, they can still come under attack by demons. Being indwelled by Christ, evil cannot possess them, but it won't stop evil from harassing and trying to control them. Read Ephesians 6 and understand the daily battle.

Now, think of how evil might form an attack. Most of us have seen the Wizard of Oz movie where the witch points with her hands and throws off bolts of electricity or fire to attack her victims. This is what the bible would call "fiery darts of the evil one" (Ephesians 6:16). Those fiery darts attack us in our brain and stimulate thoughts that seem to come from nowhere. You cannot see the fiery darts as they approach, but you may have a negative thought or suggestion come to mind without reason.

Consider the brain. It is an organ, an electrochemical device. If you shot electrical impulses into a brain you might stimulate certain memories and thoughts. Consider Satan and his ability to accompany surgeons and neurologists during their discussions, autopsies, classes and surgeries. Satan knows the human brain better than anybody and can train his workers to follow along and learn. What if they know how to badger you, a simple alcoholic? Do you think they would leave you alone for long?

People, particularly alcoholics, have bizarre thoughts that come out of nowhere. While we can speculate endlessly as to what internal malfunction might cause such a thought, as spiritual people, it is also reasonable to consider evil as a source of attack.

For the sake of helping you, indulge us and assume we know what we are talking about. We are not seeing Satan behind every bush, but we also shouldn't pretend he doesn't exist. If we will simply assume that God's word is true, we can find ways to protect ourselves from any external spiritual influences.

Let's face it. It isn't just the unseen enemy that can come after us. Most of us have had some kind of venomous attack made against us somewhere along the line by flesh and blood humans. Those attacks always disturb us, sometimes deeply and permanently, but we may be receiving similar attacks from the unseen world around us and not even give it a second thought. We just chalk up our difficulties to our own mental infirmities. We might mistakenly close our mind to the prospect of evil attacking us because it seems a strange thing for us to even consider. If we are closed minded on the subject, we are easier prey.

Alcoholics might more readily understand and believe what we are saying. If they have gone very far down the road of self destruction they have encountered many ghouls within their own mind. They may have nagging thoughts of suicide or revenge. They may carry a grudge far too long. They may have irresistible impulses and act irrationally. They are then likely to drink in an attempt to quench the fire. Again, it is like pouring gas on the fire in hopes of putting it out. Instead it only gets worse.

What must eventually happen for the alcoholic, and perhaps for the family around him, is a hedge of protection must be gained. It can only come from God, but God is not necessarily going to give you such a hedge if you don't acknowledge Him with your ways. Many of us want God to protect us so that we can do what we want. We pray to Him like Santa Claus. We want this and that. We make bargains with Him as if we are calling the shots.

We need to remember that God doesn't play favorites (Acts

10:34) and that He wants us to be bowed down and humble before Him (Proverbs 15:33). He will somehow crush our foolish pride otherwise. If we want His help, we must be willing to do our part to keep ourselves and our family safe from evil.

Many people refuse to do it. People love their sinful lives and self-indulgences. We can offer little hope to those who want the world more than they want a relationship with God. We would only ask that you pray about this and consider carefully.

If you are committed to finding relief from alcoholism for your family, if you want to be free of the influence of evil, it is important to pursue a plan of action. For the alcoholic, it means stopping drinking, no matter what. If the alcoholic doesn't want to quit, let him find his bottom, even if it takes him down very dangerous roads. He might then come to his senses with God, and hopefully the family will be prepared to support that authentic effort.

Ultimately, the alcoholic will need to get involved with a fellowship or ministry that will help him work through his mental aberrations. There are choices both secular and Christ centered. The important thing is to know what help the family will provide when the alcoholic becomes ready. There are concepts here that will help you make good decisions.

As for the rest of the family, while the alcoholic is still flirting with disaster, the family must protect itself from the effects of disaster. The family may want to take life insurance on the alcoholic if the policy can be bought without engaging the assistance of the alcoholic. The same goes with protecting family finances and trying to keep family business in order. Sometimes an intervention is needed wherein the family confronts the alcoholic and tells him they are taking over to help keep the family safe. It is important not to demand the alcoholic get sober, or say "We are doing this until you get better." Just take over and let him earn his way back without any promise of how or when that might happen.

If the alcoholic is committed to self loathing, he will continue down the path of suicide on the substance abuse installment plan. The family needs to be emotionally prepared to bury him. Even so, there are other measures to take that will hopefully keep the family safe.

Evil creeps in everywhere when there is a wide open door created by alcoholism. It could come in the form of unsavory friends, weapons, extramarital affairs, pornography, family violence, or ongoing loud arguments and threats. Evil then comes right into the family and makes itself at home. Sons might want to fight their father. Wives may want to murder their husbands. Father-in-laws may want to hire somebody to teach their alcoholic son-in-law a lesson.

Avoid allowing this to happen every step of the way. Carefully read Ephesians 6 again and make it a daily habit and daily prayer among you. Pray with or without the alcoholic but don't let them know you are praying for them to quit drinking. The spiritual battles are bigger than just alcoholism. If the alcoholic suspects you are trying to "fix" him behind his back and are praying about him, it will only distance him further and prod him to deeper paranoia and denial. Conversely, if the alcoholic wants desperately to quit drinking but cannot seem to do so, it is okay if they are fully engaged in the prayer life of the family.

Adult members of the household should contact Al-Anon and start attending meetings at least once weekly. Teenage children can often attend Alateen at the same time. Try to find meetings where A.A. meets simultaneously. We have seen cases where the alcoholic starts wondering about Al-Anon and starts to go along. Sometimes that is how the alcoholic joins Alcoholics Anonymous.

Church should be something you attend even if the alcoholic speaks against it. Get an appointment with the pastor or a pastoral care worker at church. Also locate an alcoholism counselor and get suggestions for who might be available for an intervention if the opportunity should arise.

If the alcoholic gets physical and shows signs of violence, retreat into a safe room. If he assaults somebody physically or breaks down a door, get out of the house (if you can) and call the police. If violence is imminent, move out and have somebody the alcoholic knows check on the house. At least have somebody accompany you if you need to return to the house and it should be somebody that will know how to respond if a difficult situation should arise.

It is sometimes necessary to get a restraining order to keep the alcoholic out of the home, especially when children live in the home. Court Orders for Protection should be used sparingly. The reason is simple. Once you have requested a restraining order, the marriage is in deep trouble and the alcoholic is not likely to find a way to make peace easily.

A one-time tirade of non-interpersonal violence is not good, but it might be an acceptable threshold without calling the police. An emergency call to 911 is always indicated if there is physical violence, including shoving or involuntary embraces, taking children hostage in a room, displaying a weapon, or a credible threat of serious injury. You can even train the children on this subject, being careful not to stir fear in them. Tell them their alcoholic parent is sick right now and going through a bad time, explain in simple terms that it is important to pray for the alcoholic and love him, while it is also important to keep the family safe. Kids will understand and it will help them feel safer and more confident in most cases.

Also share with children that their alcoholic parent loves them but could hurt them if the alcoholic is not in his right mind. Explain the violence thresholds and tell them that any time you become disabled or can't speak with them that they should call the police or run and get help.

Hopefully, none of these situations will arise, but if they do, better to be prepared. To be sure that you are not alarming your children unnecessarily, we would suggest you only have these discussions with children when there has been some display of dangerous behavior that the children have witnessed. You don't want the children to think you might be turning against the alcoholic parent without good justification. You also don't want to disturb the innocence of a child's life without good cause.

Children are often very protective of the sick alcoholic parent and will be slow to hold them accountable. They are inclined to withdraw when there are problems and they sometimes will live in a created fantasy and pretend that everything is fine when it is clearly not the case. It is important to calmly and lovingly keep a child updated with conversations that meet their maturity level. They need to know the truth and learn how to adjust instead of pretend, but you don't want to create any unnecessary drama. Kids typically feed off of any drama they have around them and run with it.

Finally, regarding evil, there are many ministries nowadays that help families identify things in our homes and in our behaviors that are offensive to God. If we are quite serious about the well being of our family, it would serve us well to keep an open mind toward these types of services, particularly since they are inexpensive and more widely available than ever. It is a rather recent phenomenon in the church to consider how we offend God. Until now we have mostly just sinned, repented and asked for forgiveness.

The emphasis now, more than ever, is on true repentance, i.e. change that occurs at a deeper level within us. When this kind of real world repentance takes place within us, we don't act more holy or simply appear different to the people around us. We become more devout and unwilling to endanger our peace with God. We find that we only want to live within His grace and so we start to abandon those things which no longer serve that relationship.

We may find we no longer enjoy our romantic fantasies. Men may lose interest in pornography, not because they might get caught with it, but because it cheapens their desires for a godly woman. Women might quit reading romance novels, ridding their hearts of unrealistic expectations that no man will ever match. Children will start to find contentment with what they have instead of always wanting something new and fascinating before they will consider themselves happy.

How does all of this revolutionary change occur? It begins with an awareness of our ungodly behaviors, increases to a point of a raised consciousness of our corrupt desires, and culminates in us asking for God's help to overcome these worldly desires. This is how we overcome evil. We give it no platform to rest and no time to build a nest.

When we become aware of an unhealthy desire, we simply ask God to help us remove this shortcoming and we continue to resist and pray until the desire seems to tire of tempting us. It may come back again later, with even more cunning, but if we are diligent and keep making the choice that favors God, He will continue to strengthen us and bless us for our faithfulness in following Him.

For many of us this sounds unrealistic. We somehow conjure in our minds that we could never do this, that it isn't practical. We think we don't have time to stop and pray every few minutes, and perhaps we feel we really don't want to change if it is that much trouble.

We may want to limit how much of our selfish desires we have to relinquish. We might wonder how good we have to be just to get sober, or just to have our husband quit cheating on us. Then, once we attain that goal, we can move on and return to our comfortable lifestyle again. We somehow think that God can't see through our charades, so we pretend to be faithful and hope things go well, all the time really just trying to get by and get our own way.

We forget that Jesus knew what people were thinking even before He was resurrected and returned to heaven. Read Luke 5:22 and Luke 6:8. God always knows our hearts whereas evil cannot read your mind. God is everywhere and sees all things whereas Satan and his demons are finite and can only be in one place and only see and hear what is around them. Now, it is true that Satan and his demons are very clever and are good at listening in and watching us when we think we are alone. They see our weaknesses and know how to play upon them, but they cannot read our minds.

The sins we think are secret are cataloged and used against us when evil comes calling to tempt us. Sometimes we have very little defense and our mind is tortured and we feel compelled to act out sinfully.

We have found that praying out loud is often a good defense against evil. It puts the angels on notice that you are in need of help and they are sometimes in a position to oblige. Our prayers also put the demons on notice that we are calling on God for help and that we are not going to be bullied. James 4:7 tells you to humble yourself before God, resist the devil and he will flee from you. Notice that crying out loud for help is a great way to humble yourself before God and put the angels and demons on notice. Know that you are not alone, confirm your relationship with God as Master, and you will find fulfillment and will have nothing to fear from the dark side of life.

Despite the difficulties around you, you may want to pray for a hedge of protection for you and your family. There may be family members who are working against the very concept, but having the hedge of protection for those who honor the Lord within your family might be the precious beginning of a spiritual overhaul for the entire clan. We would suggest that Psalm 91 (NLT) might be good to read out loud among the active believers in your home or in your life.

> [1] Those who live in the shelter of the Most High
> will find rest in the shadow of the Almighty.
> [2] This I declare about the LORD:
> He alone is my refuge, my place of safety;
> he is my God, and I trust him.
> [3] For he will rescue you from every trap
> and protect you from deadly disease.
> [4] He will cover you with his feathers.
> He will shelter you with his wings.
> His faithful promises are your armor and protection.
> [5] Do not be afraid of the terrors of the night,
> nor the arrow that flies in the day.
> [6] Do not dread the disease that stalks in darkness,
> nor the disaster that strikes at midday.
> [7] Though a thousand fall at your side,
> though ten thousand are dying around you,
> these evils will not touch you.
> [8] Just open your eyes,
> and see how the wicked are punished.
>
> [9] If you make the LORD your refuge,
> if you make the Most High your shelter,
> [10] no evil will conquer you;
> no plague will come near your home.
> [11] For he will order his angels
> to protect you wherever you go.
> [12] They will hold you up with their hands
> so you won't even hurt your foot on a stone.
> [13] You will trample upon lions and cobras;
> you will crush fierce lions and serpents under your feet!
>
> [14] The LORD says, "I will rescue those who love me.

I will protect those who trust in my name.
[15] When they call on me, I will answer;
I will be with them in trouble.
I will rescue and honor them.
[16] I will reward them with a long life
and give them my salvation."

"Look, Bob, I'm raking my leaves like a 'regular guy.' Want to come over later for a beer?"

Spiritual Encouragement

Be aware that alcoholism is a subtle foe and will raise its ugly head as soon as you relax and think you have it made. This is true for the entire family, not just the recovering alcoholic. Many have failed as they became confident of their spirituality and let up on their spiritual practices.

What follows are spiritual matters that you may choose to meditate upon as you progress. There are many truths in the Kingdom that are not often discussed and they will benefit you when you are ready. Indeed, as you grow more focused on the presence of the Spirit of God in your life, you will find that you must delve deeper into your relationship with Him. May those who are called to hear listen.

We are made in God's image but He is not male or female. God is a Spirit and those who worship Him must do so in spirit and in truth (John 4:24). We are made in His image and we are little creators who have the power of choice.

All of our power and direction should come from God. In John 17: 20-23 (NLT) Jesus talks about us being one with Him as He prays this prayer to the Father:

> "I am praying not only for these disciples but also for all who will ever believe in me through their message. I pray that they will all be one, just as you and I are one—as you are in me, Father, and I am in you. And may they be in us so that the world will believe you sent me. I have given them the glory you gave me, so they may be one as we are one. I am in them and you are in me. May they experience such perfect unity that the world will know that you sent me and that you love them as much as you love me."

It is not necessary to try to grow closer to God. Jesus Christ is already in us, so we don't need to grow closer, we need to grow more familiar. Think about it like a husband and wife.

When they are in each other, they reflect perfect unity. In the

Old Testament, God uses the Hebrew word "yada" to describe sex. When Adam "knew" Eve and a child was born, the word "knew" is the Hebrew word "yada." But the Hebrew word "yada" is also used to describe any intimacy between people.

God has constantly used the husband-wife relationship to display what unity looks like. Genesis 2:24 and Mark 10:8 both tells us that "the two shall become one." It is the same as what Jesus is preaching in John 17:20-23 about unity in the Kingdom. We are to find a way to put ourselves aside and dwell in the eternal power of God. We rightfully seek full reunification with the Spirit of God.

This is quite the opposite of our natural flesh desires and it is also the opposite of what Satan wants. Even our culture screams out for rugged individualism that contradicts God's spoken desire for perfect unity among us. Let's face it, we cannot be Mr. and Mrs. Special and still be humble before God. But we can do special things as directed by God and experience the most special of feelings.

In Isaiah 30:21 God tells us that He is the voice behind our ear telling us whether to turn right or left. This is a reminder that it is God's path we must seek in order to be fulfilled. We may strive for recognition and significance while here on earth, but the applause of mankind is as clanging cymbals when compared to the pleasure of being just a small part of God's perfect and majestic symphony.

Some superstars in life know this and pay tribute to God and find peace in their fame because they don't rely on the fame to pleasure them. They are simply pleased to be used by God in such a way that they can bring favor upon His name. Other people glorify their own effort and, like gladiators in the arena of life, want nothing more than the adoration of the people. At the end of the age, those who glorified God will be favorably rewarded and will be superstars in heaven whether or not they received recognition while on earth. In turn, those who sought favor on earth will have little reward in heaven, if they should even have the hand of grace bring them there.

In three of the four Gospels we are told that the first shall be last. It is a paradox that God wants us to realize that the way up is down. Like He loves His Son, He loves us for our pure humble nature, if we have developed humility. But, like a good parent, He will also resist us in our pride and selfishness.

What made Jesus perfect was that He was God, but what made Him successful on earth and brought glory to the Father was His willingness to overcome the flesh while on earth, His desire to fulfill every direction from the Father, and His undeserved sacrifice on the cross. While Jesus lost His worldly life, He showed us the power and glory of God in the resurrection of the Spirit and the creation of the new and glorified body.

Are we to also forfeit our life? The answer is yes, but only in the way the Spirit instructs us. We are not to seek martyrdom. We, pridefully, are not to exert our will to quit drinking. We are not to do any spiritual act in our own power. We are to align ourselves with the Spirit of God as best we can each day and then act in His behalf in good conscience.

God commands us to not be a drunk, so we obey humbly by choosing not to drink, asking for His strength and thus overcoming the grape. For the family of the alcoholic, God commands us not to appease evil or be a stumbling block for good. For all concerned, this means we must forfeit our lives to God. But it also means our lives are going to be fulfilled by God.

There are many of us that are not willing to entrust our lives to God. We think He is going to somehow have us standing on a street corner handing out leaflets or performing some other task to which we might object. We miss the simple truth that if God is our creator then He knows what will best please us.

God isn't like a teacher who is trying to test us to see how smart or wise we are. He loves us more than any teacher and His tests are designed to draw us nearer (Genesis 22:1-2). Nor is he like a coach who is trying to get us to do our physical best; a coach cannot strengthen and propel you to victory. He is the Author of our life, our very Creator. He knows us better than we know ourselves. Think about it.

Pretend for a moment that you are a magnificent expensive automobile. The manufacturer is your creator and has prepared a special book that tells all about how you operate. This owner's manual tells how to maintain yourself, what your limitations are, and how to properly use your equipment. It tells you what kinds of paths are safe and which are severe and high maintenance. But there is one thing this special book does not tell you.

The bible is your owner's manual and it tells you everything you need to know except perhaps the most important thing—what is your specific place to go and your specific thing to do. No car manufacturer knows where in the world you might drive your car, but God knows exactly what He recommends for each creation. The challenge is for you to be quiet enough to hear the voice behind your ear, the voice that tells you to turn left or right.

It may sound boring to always do what God wants, but after doing it you will come to find out that it is the greatest high. It is better than any drug or romantic experience. We would like to testify before you now that there is no high like the Most High.

Getting in touch with the Most High seems difficult for us. We pray and don't get results so we tend to just pray mechanically and not expect too much. We forget that we dwell in unity with God and that our prayer is not supposed to be a recitation or list of things we want... it is supposed to be us pouring out our heart to Him (Psalm 62:8 and Luke 18:9-14). We mistakenly treat God like a vending machine. Put in your prayer and select your prize. Sometimes it works and sometimes it doesn't, or so we think. The problem is that we pray selfishly and are not aligned spiritually with God when we pray. Most of our prayers are in the flesh.

Prayer is a good start to communicating with God. It pours out our heart and confesses our inadequacies and establishes Him as Lord and Master, at least if done properly. We might also share our heartaches and desires for the people around us and pray for healing for our loved ones, all of which is fine when we are in tune with God.

But there is still more. Once we have said our peace with God it is important for us to stop and listen and see what God has to say to us. This is the lost art of Christian meditation. Remember the voice behind our ear that tells us to turn right or left. Really, when is the last time you felt God was directing your path? It takes a trained and sensitive ear to hear the Master, and the Master's voice is unmistakable in our lives.

In John 10:25-30 (NLT), Jesus lays out the case clearly. "I have already told you, and you don't believe me. The proof is the work I do in my Father's name. But you don't believe me because you are not my sheep. My sheep listen to my voice; I know them, and they follow me. I give them eternal life, and they will never perish. No one can snatch them away from me, for my Father has given them to me, and he is more powerful than anyone else. No one can snatch them from the Father's hand. The Father and I are one."

The truth is that God is constantly directing the steps of the righteous (Psalm 37:23) even though a man may fall at times. It is important for us to seek God's kingdom first and His righteousness, and all these things shall be added unto us (Matthew 6:33). In seeking God's kingdom, we are first to seek to be good subjects. A good subject is loyal to the King, so God wants us to love Him with all of our heart.

But He also wants us to seek His righteousness. Notice that we are not to be righteous in our own power. It is not "our" righteousness. It is "His" righteousness. The way we must pursue His righteousness is to first show our loyalty to Him by disavowing our own righteousness.

Then we are to "seek" His righteousness. Notice it doesn't say to "act" righteous or "be" righteous. We are to pursue God, not catch Him as if He were our prey. He isn't to be kept in a nice little box or on a shelf where we can keep an eye on Him. He is to be worshipped humbly and allowed to have His way in our life.

Some of us try to imitate Christ, but we cannot play God, even in our own lives. Nor does He need us as spiritual advisors. The best we can do is come humbly to Him like children and be grateful that we are allowed to live under His loving guidance and protection.

Then what happens? He tells us that then all "these things" shall be added unto us. What is He talking about? Read Matthew 6 and you will see that Jesus was talking about the daily needs we have for sustenance. God wants us to have confidence that He is watching over us, that He loves us, and that He doesn't want to deny us. Our job is to acknowledge Him as Lord and glorify Him as we live.

The more we can muster the spiritual courage to align with God, the more He can thrill us with His presence. One way to align with God is to meditate upon His word. Meditation is mostly now a lost art in Christianity that needs to be revived. Meditation can be described as reflection or deep study. It is the process of putting aside worldly concerns and focusing on spiritual concerns. While prayer can be described as pouring out your heart to God, meditation can be described as drinking in God's heart. Try drinking that for a change!

Pick a bible verse that resonates with you. Farris likes to use Psalm 46:10 (KJV), "Be still, and know that I am God." When you are alone, recite the verse out loud, not silently. Memorize it. If you are counted among the faithful, He will help quiet your mind and calm you. This is why Farris calls upon God to help him be still. He has learned that his own mind can be his worst enemy.

This is often the case for alcoholics. Alcoholics feel the need to self-medicate because they are overwhelmed in their minds by life problems. Those troubles often run uncontrollably through their mind like a broken record. The stress of having worries and constant reminders of failure is just too much.

But it is also true for many of us. A mind that runs rampant can be a terrible and constant distraction. Stilling one's mind is also one of the results of Christian meditation.

A straightforward way to meditate is to first pick a location that is quiet and where you are not expecting disruptions. Make yourself comfortable as you sit and relax. Have your palms facing outward or upward. Quietly and slowly pray your verse out loud. Breathe evenly and ever more slowly, focusing on the meaning of the words. Continue more deliberately and softly. Soon you should begin to experience the rising of the Spirit of God from within you. Wait for God to start to create feelings around you and within you.

You might experience some sensations around your hands or

your head or your feet. You might also experience a rising up feeling within your body. Some people report feeling lighter than air at times.

Whatever physical sensations you have or don't have is not really important. The sensations are simply a confirmation from the Spirit of God that He is there with you and that you can count on Him. The real prize is that your mind is starting to work properly. It will become still for most of us.

If you are a person who just cannot seem to meditate upon God's word, don't feel alone. You should continue faithfully to meditate upon His word all the same because you will eventually get the promised results of a still mind. If you have distractions in your body or mind when you meditate, you should focus on those and use your meditation time to become very aware of those feelings. Distractions will often disappear once they get the attention they want. Then you will be able to meditate at a deeper and more beneficial level.

Farris remembers how difficult it was for him when he got sober at age 31. He couldn't handle lengthy prayer, much less meditation. He was far too distracted by every little thing. He was like a child that couldn't sit still, but his restlessness was inside his mind instead of his body.

His challenge, earlier in sobriety, was to find healthy distractions and focus on them instead of allowing his mind to be hounded by negative thoughts. His inability to initially be able to focus on spiritual tasks was the result of an untrained spiritual mind. He needed to start with something more basic than meditation.

Many people even have trouble praying, particularly people who have been living like the devil. A trick some people use is to put their shoes under their bed so that they have to get on their knees to retrieve them and put them away. While they are there they just go ahead and say a few words.

God is easy to find and makes Himself readily available once a lost sheep seeks Him again earnestly. Keep in mind that a newly recovering alcoholic has been living without a sound mind or godly purpose for an extended period of time. They have forgotten how to live a sane life. They are likely to have difficulty focusing on the reality of life around them, much less the seemingly vague presence of God within them.

Occasionally we will find somebody God restores to mental health quickly. Many people have taken those blessings and assume that God will always do that for them. Unfortunately, people who easily find sobriety are more likely to drink again. It is a grave mistake to think that God is at our beck and call. Certainly He hears our prayers but He is under no obligation to put up with our "on again, off again" childish spiritual ways. We have seen many men die who continued to tempt God.

The alcoholic who claims Christ but continues to tempt God by drinking is showing his defiance and is worse than a unbeliever. Let's review Matthew 11:20-22 (NLT) to see what Jesus was saying to the hometown crowds that had witnessed His miracles: "...if the miracles I did in you had been done in wicked Tyre and Sidon, their people would have repented of their sins long ago, clothing themselves in burlap and throwing ashes on their heads to show their remorse. I tell you, Tyre and Sidon will be better off on judgment day than you."

These Israelites were God's people, had seen His prophets, and watched as Jesus performed miracles among them in behalf of the Father. Yet they continued to be proud and defiant. For them it would be worse than for those who never saw God.

The alcoholic who has had an intervention from God and later thrown away his sobriety is also in grave danger. God may take His hand off of them and let them live as they please. In 2 Timothy 3:1-9, we read about counterfeit faith. In 2 Corinthians 13:5-7, Christians are warned about continuing to sin. In Revelation 3:16, Jesus spits out lukewarm believers.

This is the worst thing that could happen to any of us. Mostly we work hard to get the things we want and expect to be blessed because of our hard work. When God doesn't give us our selfish heart's desires, we mumble and complain. We are also tempting God. The Israelites did the same thing.

In Exodus, we read the Israelites were in the barren desert for forty years because of their unbelief. God would not allow them into the Promised Land because of that unbelief. God uses this story as a prime example of the results we may well get when we are stubborn and ungrateful.

Read chapter eleven in the book of Numbers. The people were receiving manna from heaven. God was providing the food they needed for sustenance on a daily basis. They then complained about the lack of variety of the food, even though they would have starved in the desert without it. They even longed to return to Egypt because their desire for a variety of foods was more important than their freedom.

Similarly, the sober alcoholic who doesn't respect God's blessings might become bored in sobriety and want more. He may think he deserves something special for staying sober. He may want a new girlfriend, a better job, or some public recognition. At some point, if God doesn't bless the sober alcoholic the way the alcoholic thinks he should be blessed, the alcoholic may develop resentment and drink again.

The problem is that he may never come back. God is not to be mocked or tempted. Those of us who ignore the Source of our blessings may lose what little we have. Luke 12:48 tells us that to whom much is given, much is expected, but the alcoholic may have unreasonable expectations and an ungrateful heart. He may think he is doing God a favor by staying sober.

God just wants us to acknowledge Him in our life. Is that too much to ask? We say thank you to the clerk at the store, to a friend who listens to us, and to our family when they provide help. Even though God provides all of our needs, do we stop to reflect on that and thank Him each day?

Sometimes it is just too difficult for us to pray and thank God because our minds are caught up in the whirlwind of life. That is why it is so important for all of us, and is particularly urgent for the alcoholic, to regain focus and stop the mind from running wild with every distraction.

Getting our life aligned with God will also start to straighten out our crooked thinking. Romans 8:6 tells us that the mind controlled by the Spirit is life and peace. Doesn't that sound wonderful, but perhaps also a little vague?

We think of our life as belonging to us. It is my life, my room, my clothes, my food, my job, my free time, etc. We are so entrenched in our ownership of life that we fail to see the hand of God at work. Letting God start to control our mind may sound weird, but it works. You just have to ask Him to do it and then give Him the opportunity!

Think about it. Hasn't it been your best thinking that has gotten you in some of the most unsavory situations? Don't we trust God to do what is best for us? Then why hold out on Him?

When it comes to our lives, we are only the custodians, not the owners. God is the founder, creator, owner and director. We are His servants. It would do us well when we come into the Kingdom to wear a sign around our neck for a month that says, "Under New Management." That would serve as a constant reminder to us and also to the world around us.

In some Christian circles it is customary to ask people if they have been "saved." Instead, let's ask people if they have been "slaved." In other words, are they still master of their own life, or have they become a slave to Christ? That is a pretty unsettling notion for most people. Read 1 Corinthians 7:22. Some people are not ready to let God have his way with them. They may want to stop short of being sold out to God and say, "Perhaps we had better just survive our alcoholic life and hope for the best."

People caught up in any ongoing sinful lifestyle cannot see that they are already slaves in the flesh and in bondage to the ways of the world. Read these excerpts from John 8:31-47 (NLT):

Jesus said to the people who believed in him, "You are truly my disciples if you remain faithful to my teachings. And you will know the truth, and the truth will set you free... everyone who sins is a slave of sin... For you are the children of your father the devil, and you love to do the evil things he does...He has always hated the truth, because there is no truth in him. When he lies, it is consistent with his character; for he is a liar and the father of lies...And since I am telling you the truth, why don't you believe me? Anyone who belongs to God listens gladly to the words of God. But you don't listen because you don't belong to God."

People like to think they are in control of their life even when sin has become their master. Alcoholics are an extreme example of how we become enslaved to sin, and yet they will typically recoil from any suggestion that they be a slave to Christ. The rebellion within us is so great. The only solution is repentance, an absolute turnaround. The lurking reservations in our mind will otherwise become tomorrow's obsessions.

Maybe you are getting discouraged that this spiritual path looks steep, rocky and narrow. This course of action may seem like spiritual supervitamins you have to take every hour, when you would prefer to just try some "one a day" vitamins. If the thought of all of this change is too challenging, please relax and know that we are trying here to offer spiritual encouragement across the spectrum. Hopefully it will ease your mind to know there is no danger that any of us will become perfect anytime soon, nor will we float off to heaven. There is plenty of room for improvement all around the globe.

The point is that we wouldn't want you to be ignorant of the truth even though you might not feel qualified to live at an extreme spiritual level right now. Please know that God has you right where you belong and that your spiritual growth will be directed by Him as you go. But you have to seek.

Sometimes it is hard to seek because we are in such turmoil. At times when one cannot seem to find any desire for things spiritual, there are world alternatives that can help keep us safe. Farris likes to jokingly say that he has two brain cells left after all the hard living he enjoyed as a youth. One is labeled "Humility" and the other "Service." Whenever he is tempted to take control of deteriorating conditions around him, when frustration is prompting him toward rage, he has to take a break, move very carefully, and do something terribly simple.

Farris recalls when he first got sober telling God, "I don't care if I live in a Salvation Army bunk bed and do nothing but sweep floors the rest of my life, I just want to feel better about myself." That reminder is simplified to the two-step concept of Humility and Service.

Since Farris is not allowed to leave his family and move into a men's mission, he does the next best thing. He finds a safe task, like doing dishes or sweeping or taking out the trash. That simple task helps him stay humble and busy as he serves those around him.

Another quick antidote for self-pity is calling others on the phone. It is best even to find somebody who might also need a friend. Having phone numbers of people in 12-step programs or church groups can save you, at a critical moment, from destructive behavior. But you are not likely to make a phone call if you have not spent time doing so in the recent past. So, it is always good to keep in touch with people on a casual basis so that you are comfortable calling them when you need to.

We have also supplied some chapters at the end of the book (*Spiritual Tools for Your Toolkit* and *Reminders*) to help you stay focused or find a good word when you need one. It is important for you to develop tools that will aid you and your family.

FAiTH ANd WoRks

The book of James was one portion of the bible, along with other Christian literature, that was read by alcoholics as they gathered together before Alcoholics Anonymous had been formed. They even considered calling themselves the James Club instead of A.A. James 2:26 (KJV) is quoted in the Big Book of Alcoholics Anonymous three different times, "Faith without works is dead."

In the personal story of one of A.A.'s founders, Bill Wilson, he recalls a visit from his friend, Ebby Thatcher, who had a revolutionary spiritual experience, "Faith without works was dead, he said. And how appallingly true for the alcoholic! For if an alcoholic failed to perfect and enlarge his spiritual life through work and self-sacrifice for others, he could not survive the certain trials and low spots ahead. If he did not work, he would surely drink again, and if he drank, he would surely die. Then faith would be dead indeed. With us it is just like that."

Up to now we have focused on enlarging our spiritual lives, but it is important to know that we must engage in some activities which will require us to get out of our reading chairs. So, what are some of the works we will do?

The A.A. text suggests "self-sacrifice for others." John 15:13-14 (NLT) reminds us of the love Christ showed at the cross, "There is no greater love than to lay down one's life for one's friends. You are my friends if you do what I command."

Earlier we discussed how important it was for us to act as a "slave" to Christ, even though He considers us as a Friend. It is our deep commitment to Christ that captivates and frees us, not our obligation to be a lowly slave. We lower ourselves before Him in great love and appreciation.

It is interesting that Jesus says we are His friends if we do what He asks. Being willing to do what He asks is the qualifier. That is why it is good to consider ourselves as His slave. So, what does He ask? What will it take for the alcoholic family to experience sanity and sobriety?

Perhaps we are willing to pray and meditate or maybe we are not yet ready. Perhaps we can read through this book and discuss it among our loved ones or perhaps it is just too difficult to get through. Perhaps we can go to church and A.A. and Al-Anon or maybe we are just too intimidated by the prospect. Perhaps we don't even recognize that we are paralyzed by doubt. We might even have faith galore and even pray constantly but we just can't seem to move forward.

We might be like the father and daughter at the circus watching the bicyclist getting ready to ride across the high tightrope. We may have faith in the fact the bicyclist can ride across the high wire, but we aren't ready to trust him enough to get up on the handlebars and go with him.

But let's take a deeper look at such a scene. Let's pretend the girl looks up and asks her dad if that man can really ride across that skinny tightrope. The father says he can because he has seen it before and heard about it many times from reliable people.

The daughter then asks what will happen if he falls. The father points to the large net that would catch him if something should go wrong. He assures her the safety net has never failed. The daughter then says it looks scary but she would like to try it. The father then says it is too dangerous.

Both the father and child have faith the man can do it, but only the child trusted the safety net enough to risk the fall from high. We shouldn't fault the father who may not have an interest in being a dare devil, and the truth is that the child isn't trained to ride the high wire at the circus. The father was using prudence in suggesting it was dangerous.

So, it is okay for you to only go as far as your trust and training allows as long as you are doing your best. Strive always to put God's instructions in your life ahead of your own desires. If God doesn't appear to be speaking to you, don't let that stop you. The bible can instruct you along the path of self-sacrificial daily living with little or no inspiration, so long as you are obedient to God throughout the process. Armed with that sure knowledge, we can take risks in faith and trust God for the proper results.

So, just what is it we can do? For the alcoholic, the obvious answer is to pray for the daily power to resist temptation, center our thoughts on God, engage in daily devotions, and work with other alcoholics in recovery. For the family of the alcoholic, we must center our lives around God, pray for the power to not enable or focus on the alcoholic, engage in daily devotions, and work with other people or families that suffer from alcoholism.

It is interesting in the spiritually mature family that the daily effort of spiritual living starts to look the same among all of the family members. Some day you may be able to look back and realize that it was each person's individualistic choice of sin that separated you and made you think you were different from each other.

After years of healthy sane living you may all start to think alike, act alike and make the same good choices. You probably won't notice it at first, but if the family were to apply itself consistently for five years, you would find out that the family's ideas about alcoholism are changing from year to year.

As you leave Medical School and enter Residency, you will encounter alcoholics and you will need to diagnose them without their help... usually they're in better shape than this one.

There are two things to know:

1. You can always tell an alcoholic, and

2. Unfortunately, you just can't tell them much!

We want you to be aware that "alcoholism" is not about drinking. It is about the affliction of the family that accompanies drinking to excess. Also notice that it is called "alcohol-is-m," not "alcohol-was-m." We are not "cured" of the affliction; it is arrested every day by our allegiance within the Kingdom of God.

In turn, our sacrificial work can easily be aimed toward helping others who can benefit from our experience. Sometimes it is enough for an alcoholic to get sober and get active in church. Others feel the call to work more closely with alcoholics and their families. We have found few people enjoying a post-alcoholic life without also engaging in some kind of godly service to others.

We believe that God has allowed this affliction into your life for a reason and given you a natural way to benefit others. We are writing this book in hopes that you will carry God's message to other individuals who struggle. Perhaps you will even start a group at your church to facilitate other families!

That may seem like an impossibility right now as you struggle with your first steps in this lifelong process, but God often uses the newly saved to reach out to others. Getting into action will provide some initial common purpose for your family. Even in smaller towns, there are a variety of efforts in which you can engage that will benefit your family and the community in which you live. This is dependent, of course, on the healing process and how damaged the drinker may be.

The alcoholic, once ready to stop drinking, will need help. Hospitals, treatment centers, therapists, and churches are good options, but Alcoholics Anonymous is also important. We have found that church is sometimes a place where an alcoholic goes to "pretend" he has been cured. It is not healthy to "pretend" whatsoever...we need to engage in some serious soul searching and spiritual work.

Treatment centers, therapists and other professionals can help get us on the right path and they are also going to want to see their client involved in some form of ongoing spiritual growth. Hospitals are good for the first week of sobriety and can assist with a complicated detoxification if needed.

We favor getting the professional assistance needed first, if any is needed. It is always good to get a doctor's opinion as soon as possible so that the alcoholic and his family have confidence in the medical condition of the alcoholic.

Often times there are complications which may fuel frustration and create feelings of desperation. The sooner these complications are identified, the sooner the family can look for a solution together. It is important for the loved ones to also be involved in this process if the alcoholic will allow it. This way the family will be able to be supportive and aware of things that might affect them all.

For instance, if the alcoholic has become diabetic (not an uncommon occurrence), the family will have financial hardships and new meal planning considerations. The alcoholic may not like the idea of admitting that he has these new conditions as a result of his alcoholism. Perhaps he will be embarrassed or too proud to admit this additional defeat in his life.

There is little the family can do if the alcoholic is not doing a good job of sharing information about his condition. It may not help to confront him at the risk of pushing him away. Sometimes it takes many months for an alcoholic to start to trust the family even though the family will insist there is nothing fueling any distrust. This may or may not be the case, but it is irrelevant. Each member in the family must work with their own perceptions or misperceptions as best they can and the physical effects of alcohol on the body and mind are very slow to leave.

Once the detoxification and medical issues are handled and the alcoholic is back in the community, there are choices the alcoholic will want to make. He suddenly has concerns that have been ignored until now. Many times we have seen alcoholics come into recovery and want to make up for lost time. The family may have a substantially similar desire.

Everybody is anxious to return to a healthy way of living and to enjoy the new freedom the family has available. There is no longer a drunken stranger in the home! But everybody also needs to know and remember that stopping drinking is only the beginning.

Trying to hurry up and act normal will often backfire. The alcoholic has become accustomed to handling life's twists and turns by drinking through them. He is not going to suddenly have better coping skills in early sobriety. Remember, drinking was his solution, not his problem. It was his way of dealing with life and those thoughts are likely to linger.

The truth is that drinking was typically more a problem for the loved ones. As the alcoholic enjoyed the carefree lifestyle of drinking away his worries, the family suffered. It is thus natural for the family to want to feel warm and fuzzy again once the problem of drinking is removed.

But this is an unrealistic assessment of the situation. What the family now has is a raving sober alcoholic who has no outlet for his emotions. Many families find it difficult to survive the "sobering up" process. Too many hurt feelings and ugly arguments may ruin what could otherwise be a slow and steady recovery process.

That is why it is important for the newly sober alcoholic to have some ongoing outlet where he can process his emotions and thoughts. As stated before that could be a number of different environments. For the long haul, for the budget conscious family, church groups, A.A. groups, Al-Anon, and Alateen may offer the best alternatives for all concerned. Many other community programs are subject to the funding whims of government but they can sometimes provide direction toward additional helpful resources.

The greatest advantage of community based groups is they offer empathetic souls who are in similar situations. It is a bit like being on a lifeboat with other survivors after a storm at sea. You now have a group that not only provides emotional support and understanding, but you also have a place where you can be of service to others. This makes community based groups a great opportunity for those people who really want to experience recovery.

Please know that sobriety alone is not enough. Our family is involved more than most and we see those families who are busy in recovery enjoying their home life more fully as well. They often make themselves available to lead group meetings or meet newcomers and sponsor them into sobriety. This is true not just for the alcoholic, but also for the family.

Some churches have recovery ministries that can be helpful in providing a spiritual path of growth. Be careful that you don't become closed minded when it comes to options. God has created a lot of different programs, religious and secular both, for the many different kinds of people who are inside the many different circumstances and phases of life.

The critical factor for the alcoholic is not to overindulge in rest or recuperation. He needs to be up and around as best as he can, going to meetings as often as feasible, helping others as sacrificially as time and good fortune might allow. In turn, he should not squander the family's resources any longer in any way. He and the family should consult and come to some agreement that will meet the entire family's needs. It will not do for the alcoholic to turn all of his attention away from the family, and it may seem he is avoiding the family at times when he appears so anxious to be at meetings away from home.

Family feelings of being deprived of love are natural but must not be indulged. Soon enough the family will see the alcoholic naturally return to the loved ones at home as a new man, not as an actor putting on a pretend happy mask full of painful sobriety behind the scenes. The authentic spiritual growth in this new adventure of sobriety is something the whole family needs to experience. Everybody needs to do their part to help the family recover, and every part requires some action in addition to personal devotion time.

So, while the alcoholic may be working with other alcoholics or getting involved in prayer groups or bible studies, it is equally important for the rest of the family to actively engage in some process of spiritual development. Understandably, there may be some barriers in doing so.

The family may have been away from church for some time. Perhaps embarrassment drove them away. It could be that the children in the home are no longer interested in church. They too may be suffering from the alcoholism that is in the home.

The more members of the family that are willing to return to church or go to Al-Anon or Alateen, the better. Those that are resentful and don't want to participate can create a barrier that affects the whole family. Just as with the alcoholic, it will be impossible to prod the family into corrective behavior, but open family discussions where the family is able to air their issues can help.

Of course, the alcoholic will have to be ready to hear criticism, sometimes unjustified criticism. The family often feels they are innocent and have nothing to do with the problem. Whether they are right or not is irrelevant. Everybody and everything, early in sobriety, is a mess. It's just that simple, and there is little benefit that will come from harboring secret feelings of anger. Now is the time to engage the entire family together as lovingly as possible.

The family may have been "walking on eggshells" for months or years, not wanting to wake the ugly alcoholic giant. The children may have enormous resentments for how much of their innocent life has been jeopardized or ignored. They may hate the nonalcoholic parent for not protecting them and the alcoholic parent for ruining their life.

Once the alcoholic has initially cleared his head of the fog of active drinking, usually after being sober one to two weeks, it would be wise for the adults in the household to call a family meeting. The nonalcoholic adult can start the session by admitting that everybody has had a tough time and that you all need to learn to communicate again since communication has suffered in the past. Make it clear that everybody is going to get a chance to share, but that you would like for the alcoholic to go first.

It will be important for the alcoholic to be prayed up and ready for a full and humble confession, carefully avoiding details that might hurt others. He should have already done enough spiritual work to know how negatively he has impacted the family and be ready to take some flack over his misbehavior. He should also know that this first therapeutic session will be an utter failure if the alcoholic tries to engage in self-justification or blames the family for his alcoholism.

The adults will have already had a similar session between them before the entire family is invited, and the family present should be only the immediate family. This particular meeting should be geared toward healing the younger people in the family who have very little understanding of alcoholism or the process of recovery.

Children are surprisingly resilient and will understand more than we imagine. We will need to keep it simple for them, but they will soon become allies in the family effort if they believe the family has turned the corner.

Because this family meeting sets the stage for the future of the family, the alcoholic should be deeply committed to sobriety before taking this step with the family. If the alcoholic has been persuaded to participate and is just being cooperative, this meeting might serve as a trigger for a drinking binge. Also, if the alcoholic doesn't seem fully committed to sobriety, it is better to wait until they are. In any event, every adult should be a "full partner" in this meeting. The children will perceive the authenticity and feel like it is safe to share.

As the children share, hear them out and don't correct them in a way that is harsh. It is better not to correct them at all unless their understanding is so convoluted that the therapeutic value of the family meeting is at risk. Somewhere along the line it is important for the adults to express their sorrow for the family being torn apart, with the alcoholic leading the way. It is also important for the alcoholic to share what he is doing for himself to stay sober.

Once the alcoholic has shared, the other custodial adult should share. They have hurt the family in some ways as well, but they needn't try to compete with the alcoholic or pretend they have also sinned. They should share about how they may have put the alcoholic ahead of the innocent children too easily and too often. Again, avoid justifying your behavior. Cast no blame and accept no blame. Blame will only put another brick in the wall that has already divided the family for far too long.

The nonalcoholic parent also should have a plan of action and invite the family. Tell the young people that they have been impacted. Inviting them to talk about it accomplishes a couple of things. It prepares the children to know how to express difficult feelings. It relieves the children of repressed feelings and anxiety. It also prepares them to see they also need help just like their parents need help.

Now is the time to invite the children to participate in recovery. Make clear it is not their alcoholic parent's recovery in which they are participating. It is their own recovery. After they have talked about their pain they should also see how some participation in church or Alateen could be helpful.

The nonalcoholic parent should make it as fun as possible for the family to reunite and start to have some good times together. Even though your feelings may tear at you and you find it distasteful to pretend that things are getting better, act as though things are getting better. Try to forget your feelings of having been abused. Do the right and sacrificial thing for the family as best you can.

Have some ideas of the different churches or church groups and the outings that might be available. Have some phone numbers of people you can call that can understand your issues. It may be difficult to find such people, but the 12-step programs are a sure place to start. Your pastor may also be helpful in identifying resources since he is often privy to what is going on among families in your own church and may be knowledgeable about other opportunities in the community.

Now that we have taken a few actions we should be ready for more. The alcoholic can visit treatment centers and help those who don't know if they can stay sober. Even if he has only been sober a few weeks he can tell patients it is possible to get sober and they will believe him. If he is going to church he should ask the pastor how to identify men in his congregation or others that he can help. He may want to go to a recovery ministry in town and attend some A.A. meetings.

It is absolutely necessary the alcoholic identify a mentor or sponsor, preferably somebody who has experience with alcoholism. A.A. or church is the best place to find a sponsor, and that relationship should be cemented in the first few weeks of sobriety. The alcoholic must have somebody understanding in their corner who is not in the immediate family.

Always have mentors or sponsors of the same sex. Putting aside any potential for misconduct, it is important for the alcoholic and the sponsor to have common issues and feelings. Being of the same sex is a good way to avoid jealousy or miscommunication, while providing a sounding board for sensitive issues that might be difficult to share with a member of the opposite sex.

While working with a sponsor, and in addition to making himself available to help those who are still suffering, the alcoholic should also take up a firm plan of spiritual development. Most recovery based ministries have "steps" or processes they have their participants go through. The alcoholic must not say he doesn't need to do these steps. That is a lie, he is still in denial, and he is not sufficiently invested to stay sober.

Many times people won't feel the need to participate in ministries or programs. They reason that they are comfortable and doing well as they are. What they fail to see is their future need. They can't predict that they are going to have a flat tire, a bad day, an argument, or get fired. Sure they may be spiritually fit and comfortable today, but what is their insurance for tomorrow?

An unwillingness to participate in a healthy plan for spiritual development may be a sign the person is not ready to stay sober. Perhaps pride is keeping them from admitting they need help. They might fear public humiliation. Maybe they are just lazy.

Whatever the excuse may be, God will not allow us to sit comfortable in life, avoiding conflict. He will surely give us opportunities for growth. The only way to be sure we are ready to meet such challenges is to continue to allow ourselves to be challenged. If we are not working actively through spiritual processes, we are not challenging ourselves. We are like the person hoping nothing will happen to upset their apple cart.

Then, when we are comfortable but unprepared and some disturbance comes along, we are upset in a way that we are not ready to process. We haven't the tools in our spiritual tool kit to survive, we haven't the relationships with empathetic friends that care, and perhaps we haven't much instinct left for sobriety. We might wonder, "What good has sobriety done us anyway?"

The family can have similar misadventures by being lulled into compliance. They may even falter and start to recall the alcoholic's past misbehavior. They may rant and rave when the alcoholic comes home late even though he was at a meeting or at work. Logic, love and reason will not always prevail.

Like the alcoholic, if their old feelings are not being processed in a healthy environment, they may too have an emotional relapse. Unfortunately, their relapse is less obvious and sometimes difficult to catch because it doesn't have the overt symptoms of alcohol. Still the symptoms are there and the family is sure to notice even though they may not be able to see it as a lingering part of the unhealthy family dynamic.

The children are no different. If they are not actively engaged in spiritual growth they may fall back into old patterns. They may have become accustomed to stealing or manipulating to get what they want. They may purposely, and sometimes even viciously, bring up the skeletons in the family closet and rattle the bones, hoping those memories will make the parents more controllable.

If the family is working in a spiritual program that encourages introspection, many of these dangerous episodes can be avoided. If there is not a spiritual program available near you, a regular family devotion and a regular family discussion can make it easier for the family members to communicate when they hit a rough spot and need help. There are also many good workbooks that will walk the family through a 12-step process.

Yes, it is lots of work to create an environment that will facilitate good mental health in your family, but it also gets easier and more interesting over time. At first, everybody is coming in with their own hidden garbage, secrets, and expectations. It looks bleak and it is difficult to think that things will ever get better. As time goes on and the family learns more about who each other is and what everybody feels, you will find that even the children start to like the parents and relate to their experiences. This is faith in action. Be consistent and patient.

By now we hope you are convinced that your faith without works is dead. In turn, now that you have seen how much work is involved, we want to make sure you also know that "Works without faith is also dead."

Simply put, these actions, even though they are all good, if they are not alive with faith, they will not touch the lives they could have touched nor transform our own hearts with the power of God. They are like junk food, devoid of sustenance. Our empty actions that are self-directed and lacking in faith may ease our conscience but they will not change lives.

Our experience has been that faith will sometimes arrive on the heels of good actions, even actions that people do not see as works of faith. A person may be trying hard to "act right" despite the fact that they are not aware of any faith. It is interesting that even these contrived acts often are based upon a basic faith that believes in goodness.

We have seen many people find a relationship with God by doing godly things and uncovering the fact they had faith. Still, we warn against pretending or being manipulative. You must never try to impress the people around you by making yourself look better than you really are. Any insincerity in our actions, whether or not the actions benefit others, provides us no benefit.

So, don't question your faith if you have basic faith. Whatever faith you have is enough to get started. Take your little bit of faith and move in a godly direction. Our wonderful Father will take care of the rest and increase your faith as needed.

Yes! God will increase your faith because He is the Source of your faith (Hebrews 12:2). All you had to do was want faith and He has supplied it. Our best advice is to continue to long for faith and peace with God as you do the next right thing each day. It sounds simple because it is simple, so let's not complicate it. Aren't there already enough complications in life without us creating them?

Hey! Check out what my son got me for Father's Day! Sure beats the tie he gave me last year...

Alcoholic Interventions

It is a cliché to have been through a life-altering event and refer to it as a "sobering experience." Indeed, one of the most sobering things we will ever do is get sober or try to help somebody else get sober. It can literally be a matter of life and death.

The American Foundation for Suicide Prevention tells us that approximately seven percent of people with alcohol dependence die by suicide. Many more alcoholics die from diseases caused by alcohol abuse and "accidents" involving alcohol. Thirty percent of all suicides and sixty percent of all homicides are attributed to alcohol.

In any event, alcohol is clearly a killer, but even before death strikes alcohol has already stolen life away from its primary victim and everybody who cares. For worn out families who have unsuccessfully worked to see their alcoholic find recovery, death is often anticlimactic. They are almost relieved once the initial grief has passed. Still, those families always wonder if they could have done more.

One increasingly popular option is to arrange an intervention. There are five basic types of intervention: 1) Crisis Intervention, 2) Professional Intervention, 3) Impersonal Intervention, 4) Personal intervention, and 5) Orchestrated Intervention.

Crisis Intervention is opportunistic. This is sometimes an intervention arranged by God after evil has had its way. Whatever the crisis, it is marked by the alcoholic experiencing deep remorse. When the alcoholic appears both humble and pliant, his family and loved ones should be in a position to take advantage of the situation. This means that you will have established contacts with people who can help. When the time comes, you are then equipped to introduce the alcoholic who desires change with the agent for change.

For instance, if the alcoholic has a car accident the hospital might miss the fact that he created the accident himself or they may not screen for alcoholism. The alcoholic, if he is showing signs of remorse and humility, can be quietly asked if he would let you help him with a referral. The referral might be to a therapist, treatment center, minister, or A.A. friend. In any event, you can legitimately make the referral because the alcoholic is ready for the change.

Other examples of Crisis Intervention include police contacts whether or not they result in arrests, losses of jobs, alcoholic blackouts, or slips and falls. Again, the alcoholic has to perceive himself in crisis rather than us tell him he is in crisis. We are only there to provide assistance to our friend in need. Perhaps a medical condition or injury at home will provide a sufficient crisis. The whole point of Crisis Intervention is to be ready with referrals and strong encouragement when the need arises.

Do you really want to continue to ignore the elephant in the living room?

God often allows for a crisis in order to bring awareness to alcoholics. Quite often a crisis precipitates a moment of clarity. The alcoholic may even feel driven to do something different by the heightened state of affairs while in crisis. In turn, the family and loved ones, if not prepared to act in advance, may lose that opportunity as the alcoholic mind is usually quite quick to return to its wayward thinking and minimize what seemed important just a day or two earlier.

The family, not equipped in advance, may have scrambled for two days getting referrals and ideas of how to help the alcoholic. They might then come to the alcoholic with that information and find him drunk, or be disappointed that the alcoholic turns the help away, saying he can handle the situation on his own. The family is then sure to be unhappy and perhaps argumentative but they have clearly lost their chance to make a big difference. Admonishing the alcoholic about how quickly he forgets the nightmares of yesterday rarely results in a change of heart. By this time, the alcoholic needs a professional intervention, but will not be willing to admit it.

The professional intervention is conducted by a practitioner, usually a family doctor, counselor, minister, therapist, or alcoholism specialists. The professional raises the issue of drinking with the alcoholic in a way the family cannot. They have no personal attachment to the results in most cases. They can offer information and discuss issues calmly, positioning themselves to be helpful without being judgmental.

Such an intervention does not usually involve the family, but it is becoming increasingly popular for the family to be called upon soon afterward to be part of the conversation, but not necessarily an active part of the conversation. Some families even clandestinely contact the professional and offer information about the alcoholic's condition. In such cases the family and the practitioner should not hide the fact that they have communicated about the alcoholic, but don't fuel the alcoholic's potential paranoia that you are working together behind his back. It would be best in those cases if the practitioner reveals to the alcoholic that the family has been in touch with them and expressed concern.

This type of intervention allows for the gentle tones of the practitioner to penetrate the alcoholic's pride without stirring the anger the alcoholic normally might experience when anybody raises the issue of alcoholism. The professional doesn't "push" the alcoholic, and the alcoholic isn't likely to push back against a professional like they can with family. While the end result may not be immediately satisfying, the alcoholic has been confronted and will be increasingly aware of his issues. This alone is valuable.

Farris had practitioners conduct interventions on him twice before he got sober. In the 1970s and 1980s such events were not called interventions. The interventions were not prearranged and both were conducted by therapists who recognized the symptoms of alcoholism. While neither practitioner was confrontive they both were successful in raising Farris' consciousness toward his drinking even though he didn't respond right away. Still, the fact that Farris remembers them clearly thirty years later is a sign of their significance.

Some loved ones of alcoholics might be jealous that their alcoholic will more readily respond to a professional even though the loved ones have been by their side trying to help them for years. The loved ones will need to remember that they are not professionals, and that their interventions on a casual and personal basis have probably not produced results because they weren't taken seriously. In turn, trying to act more professional in our approach or trying to convince the alcoholic how much more we care only makes our efforts seem feeble.

Rather than personally engage in any kind of confrontation, consider an Impersonal Intervention. It doesn't involve direct communication with the alcoholic at all. A magazine article might be placed on your desk in a way the alcoholic might see it. Leave it there for a day or two. Note carefully that you are not to put the material in a way that is conspicuous to the alcoholic. That would be a passive-aggressive move that may well generate a hostile reaction.

There are websites you might find with interesting articles that you print. You could legitimately leave it sitting on your end table, again not positioning it to be confrontive nor bringing attention to it. Leave it there a day or two and dispose it or file it. The LORD God should be making the arrangements, not you, and you should be praying the drinker uncovers the truth but you cannot uncover it for them.

Another way to intervene impersonally is to go to 12-step meetings and read their literature quietly at home. This is the best way to show you care. You are learning to take better care of yourself and that sends a message that you are aware and concerned, but you remain undemanding. Also, the literature from Al-Anon and the fact that you are spending time away from home to go to meetings at night will likely pique the interest of the alcoholic.

When you go to a meeting, tell the alcoholic you are going to the meeting without going into a lecture. Don't make yourself attractive to go to the meeting as if to fuel jealousy. Treat it as matter-of-fact as going to the store, indicating when you will be back. This will put the alcoholic's mind at ease, remove some of the mystery, and allow him to inquire further should he be willing and able. If he shows enough interest he may want to tag along sometime and then you are free to engage in conversation. Because that could happen, it is sometimes helpful to attend an Al-Anon meeting where there is an adjacent A.A. meeting.

The important thing to remember at this low-level of impersonal intervention is that you are not involved in the intervention or communicating concerns about the alcoholic. You are doing this for yourself and the alcoholic is a witness to it and will hopefully become interested.

Then, if and when he becomes interested, you can answer the alcoholic's questions without revealing hidden motives.

Certainly, all of us with who have alcoholics in our lives will have hidden motives because we want so much for the alcoholic to find sobriety and peace, but you must restrain yourself from being emotionally attached to that result as much as possible. If you are blessed with positive results, quietly thank God, offer appropriate emotional support for positive outcomes, and do your victory dance somewhere away from the alcoholic. Again, you are supposed to be working on your issues, not his.

Still, the lines between impersonal and personal interventions easily blur at times. The Personal Intervention is a friendly process but a direct instead of indirect process. For instance, if a magazine article or website printout were suggested to the alcoholic, even lovingly, it has now become a personal intervention.

The really difficult thing for families to appreciate is that they are often the last ones that should be involved in a personal intervention. They are too close to the situation and are likely to be perceived as protecting their own interest. Also, they are the most likely people to infuse emotion into a conversation that demands self restraint, compassion, and understanding.

A Personal Intervention is best done by a friendly figure who has no personal investment. If a man's drinking buddies say he drinks too much, he may dismiss it but it will haunt him because he is likely to think highly of his peers. In turn, if he has a brother or uncle (or sister or aunt) that can approach him softly, a helpful talk might ensue. This is also true for coworkers and bosses. If alcoholism has impacted the workplace, a warning can often create an awareness and job concern in an otherwise oblivious alcoholic.

The Personal Intervention conversation should be done in the "first person," the friend or loved one talking gently and calmly about how they are concerned or impacted by the alcoholic's behavior, not just focusing on drinking. Drinking can be discussed as an apparent cause of behavior, but few alcoholics are going to be impressed to stop drinking because it bothers somebody else. In turn, if their actual behavior is unacceptable, and drinking appears to be one of the fuels that fan the flames, then the alcoholic is likely to see your point.

You should remember the alcoholic is trying not to be an alcoholic and they normally do not perceive themselves as an alcoholic. They think of alcohol as something that makes them able to cope with a stressful life, a way of avoiding boredom, or a social lubricant so they can be more at ease.

Keeping in mind that the alcoholic should never sense a conspiracy against him, it is important not to conspire. Personal interventions are events which take place between the alcoholic and the people that love him or care about his welfare. Those people may talk to each other, but there should be no manipulation of events to create artificial confrontations, even if it is for the benefit of the alcoholic. Once cooperation between friends and family occurs it is no longer a personal intervention, it is an Orchestrated Intervention.

The thought of being involved in an Orchestrated Intervention challenges us in many ways. We might feel intrusive, wondering what moral right we have to intervene. It would also be common to feel ignorant, questioning whether we are qualified to participate in such a process. We will surely feel some fear, not knowing if the intervention will produce the desired results or backfire.

There are finally some books, TV shows and literature that discuss this process, but it is still a frightfully challenging concept.   Can a family perform an intervention and have any hope of success?

The important thing to remember is not to look for success. Look for honest expressions of love. Look for feelings that are authentic, not contrived, dramatic, or designed to achieve a result.

Ruth and Farris have performed interventions for many years. We are not licensed or credentialed or degreed for this purpose, nor do we want to be. We want to operate according to God's ordination upon us to help free the captives and heal their families. So, while some people may wish to become professionals that specialize in this industry, we prefer to follow God however He leads.

This book will not teach you everything you need to know about how to do an intervention but we hope you will know enough about the process to let God lead you through the process. If nothing else, we hope you can determine when to arrange an orchestrated intervention and how to get more information about the process.

People often think of TV shows regarding Orchestrated Intervention as being the prototype of interventions, but it is the least likely intervention and the least often used. Since it is going to be orchestrated there will be much coordination. That extra effort alone makes it enormously difficult and naturally inclines us to put more emphasis on getting desired results for our heavy investment.

Some people go to great lengths and expense to orchestrate an intervention that has dismal results. That is a recipe for discouragement. If you set your expectations for results, you are sure to judge the process by the yardstick of "success" instead of the yardstick of "process."

It is paramount that everybody who is going to be involved in the Orchestrated Intervention know this is about an authentic expression of love, anger, abandonment, and concern. Forget about the results and focus on getting the message to the alcoholic right.

That is the whole point of the intervention. Everybody will be tempted to think the goal is to see the alcoholic get sober, and that would be a wonderful and ideal outcome, but it isn't guaranteed. We have found websites and programs that will give a family false hope about the probability of success, but those claims of success should be taken with a grain of salt. The bottom line is simple for an orchestrated intervention. An alcoholic will get sober when the pain of hurting their family is greater than the pain of living sober.

An Orchestrated Intervention should be arranged to get as many loved, invested and respected persons in the room as possible, each of them ready to pour their hearts out with great authenticity. They may very well want to have their talking points written out. If a participant is prone to be nervous, wordy, or judgmental, you may want to insist that everybody stick to the script they have written.

Coaching the group will be important in advance. They need to have a solid understanding of what will take place. You will want to have some advance conversations and discuss in depth what might happen during the intervention. Perhaps you will read portions of this book together or pass it around among the family in advance of the intervention.

Setting the time for an intervention is also important. You need the alcoholic to be stone cold sober when he hears from his loved ones how they have been impacted. Nobody should have booze or drugs around for a day or two before the intervention. The date and approximate time should be set. You should have a healthy sober plan for the day that will ensure the alcoholic is sober. Then comes the intervention.

The alcoholic should be in the same vehicle coming home or going to a close relative's house. Don't use a treatment center unless you have engaged an intervention specialist for the process. Still, we believe it is better done at the residence of the alcoholic. This is the battleground where they war with themselves in alcoholism and the feelings pouring out to them from the family will have a better chance at breaking through their barriers.

The intervention meeting can be known in advance as a dinner event but the excuse will not matter as much as getting everybody to agree to be there on time. Make a prearranged phone call on the way home to a family member or friend who will notify the rest of the intervention team that you are on your way home. That will tell them to be there quickly. As people arrive, let everybody get comfortable and the conversation can start as soon as the alcoholic starts to get a sense that this might be a meeting about him or her. It usually doesn't take long for an alcoholic to notice that people are acting strangely so don't hide what you are doing and whisper among yourselves.

Don't delay or stutter when it is time. One person needs to be directive and act as a facilitator. If you have a trained facilitator, allow them to speak and direct the traffic among you. No speeches are necessary and no stated intention for the purpose of the meeting is needed. Just say, "Somebody (use the name of the first person to speak) has something to say to you. Everybody gather round." Keep it simple. Let each person make clear why they are there pouring out their heart.

It is best if the alcoholic makes the decision to get sober and expresses that desire. He will already feel one of two things, anger or embarrassment. If he is angry he will be too entrenched to agree to anything anyway. He will likely stomp out in disgust and go sit on the front porch or hold his anger in and quietly insist he's not going to cooperate with the group. The purpose of the very personal and authentic sharing is to empower the alcoholic to experience enough humility to ask what he should do. It is then that "the plan" should be revealed, and not a moment sooner.

"The Plan" is what you and the intervention specialist (if engaged) have arranged to have happen when the alcoholic is ready. For some people a hospital or treatment bed may be waiting. For others a pair of A.A. members may be waiting for "the call" to take him to a meeting and follow up with him. For still others, a detoxification center may be available to help them finish "drying out."

Many states have free facilities if your alcoholic is not covered by insurance. Check with the mental health administration within your state, get referrals and call them in advance. Make clear that you are willing to accept a short-term "detox" bed if a "treatment" bed is not available. Some states have long waiting lists of people for treatment but may provide more accessible alternatives for detoxification.

If the alcoholic is really sober and has been sober for the entire day, getting them to an A.A. meeting with a couple friendly and solid A.A. members will work well most of the time. If the alcoholic wants to get sober he will stick with these new A.A. friends and do what they say. If not, he has fooled the family one more time and managed to destroy hope.

Recall earlier we were discussing the importance of a family being involved in a 12-step spiritual process for themselves, not for the alcoholic. If you have been fortunate enough to attend Al-Anon and locate a meeting that also has good A.A. ties, then you are equipped to make connections that have benefitted you and will also benefit the alcoholic when it is time. You will have become more sane, the alcoholic and the rest of the family will notice, and there is now a natural path for mutual participation and growth.

We know that sounds like a lot of effort but you have to know that you are fighting for the life of your family and your alcoholic loved one. If you were the only person to be able to save others, would you do it? This is what Jesus knew about Himself and He did it. The Father glorified that sacrifice and your sacrifice will not go without reward. Just be ready to do your absolute best and leave the results to God. Otherwise it is being done for the wrong reasons.

It is a sobering experience to think you have been successful in conducting an intervention, watched the alcoholic get sober, only to return to your own hopelessness when they return to their drinking. Make the intervention work for everybody in the room, giving each of them a chance to express their love and pain to the alcoholic. That will ensure that, even if the alcoholic returns to drinking sometime down the road, they have a new consciousness of how it affects others.

Remember Farris' recollections of interventions in his life and rest assured that you are not wasting your time. You are helping build a bright future. If nothing else, you can know that you tried everything in good conscience.

Many families will be afraid of the alcoholic's reaction and will not want to engage in an Orchestrated Intervention. They will pretend they are protecting the alcoholic and be convinced in their own mind of it. The truth is that they are killing the alcoholic and are too scared to do what is best for the alcoholic. They selfishly fear they will push the alcoholic away, but the harder reality is if they do nothing the alcoholic may die.

Few alcoholics are so hard core that they will walk away from the people that love them. Even if they do, they will come to see that you cared. Until the time their heart is softened, you need pray and be available for their prodigal return. In these unusual situations, no type of intervention will ever work, but are you ready to write them off to hell without a fight?

Every hopeless alcoholic and their hopeless family deserve one good chance to talk through their issues. Ideally, it should be a once in a lifetime event. If done with good planning and if the participants take the time to prepare, there will be some incredible results that will last a lifetime for each person in the room.

Remember me? The elephant in the Living Room?

OK guys, nice intervention... now can I come home?

Relapse Prevention and Response

An alcoholic is living in a natural state when they are drinking. Their flesh is comforted by the feeling of being high. Their coping mechanism is in place and they experience some calm, at least until the alcohol takes its toll upon their life. They then become traumatized because they have lost their last shred of hope. Even their old reliable friend, King Alcohol, has turned against them. At this moment of truth they may turn back to God, and that will be first signaled by a desire to get sober.

Conversely, an alcoholic is living in an unnatural condition when they are sober. Truly, quitting drinking requires a supernatural effort from the alcoholic. We should not then be surprised that while some alcoholics are blessed with many consecutive years of sobriety, others seem to fail periodically, almost on a cyclical basis.

Alcohol stays in the system only a short time, but the obsession in the mind can last for many years after the last drink. This is where the spiritual battleground exists, in the mind. If the alcoholic mind is not renewed by humbling oneself before God daily, the obsession and attacks by evil are likely to be successful somewhere along the line. At some point, every recovering alcoholic is going to want to get high, and if they don't have both a mental defense and spiritual approach to life, they are vulnerable.

The family has a vested interest in helping the alcoholic maintain their sobriety. The family should then also take responsibility to help create an environment that supports sobriety while being careful not to take responsibility for the alcoholic staying sober. We have discussed some of the reasons an alcoholic fails, but just what should the family do to help and how might they react when the alcoholic relapses.

It is primarily important not to take it personally when the alcoholic drinks. He may blame you, curse you, and tell you how impossible it is to stay sober around you. In turn, he may blame his boss, his ex-wife, the unemployment office, or the shoestring that broke that morning. Sometimes the alcoholic will just look at you and admit they don't know why they drank. Honestly, it doesn't matter why the alcoholic drinks except to help identify and perhaps manage triggers better in the future.

Notice that you can "manage" triggers, not eliminate them. The problem with eliminating triggers is that you cannot build an alcoholic-proof home. Other people in the family are also entitled to live and breathe. The family should not think they are helping the situation by creating an artificial environment so as not to trigger the alcoholic. In turn, it would be wise for the family not to allow for the storage or consumption of alcoholic beverages in the home, at least at first. Also, it would be a good idea if the nonalcoholics in the family refrained from coming home with booze on their breath for awhile. To take any other measures should be a point for discussion and prayer. In general, the alcoholic needn't be the center of attention or the source of our despair.

Simply put, a man chooses to take a drink. Later, when the drink takes the man, the alcoholic has then lost the power of choice because they have abandoned themselves to alcohol. They have a new king. As long as they are craving alcohol they will be a slave to it. The family has nothing to do with it.

The alcoholic has forfeited their power of choice when they drink. Once they have realized they are an alcoholic, any choice to drink thereafter is mocking God. It now takes an act of God to give them one more chance, and if they get one more chance...if their power to choose sobriety should ever return, they had better jealously guard it by submitting themselves humbly before God daily for the rest of their lives. That daily choice for God and sobriety has now become the one essential thing they must do each day. They should pray daily, constantly if needed, for God's power to survive any temptation.

So, what happens to the family when the alcoholic fails? They naturally despair, look for what triggered the event, and try to help motivate the alcoholic back to sobriety. But in spite of these overwhelming emotions and concerns, the family needs to focus on the main thing...that is not to allow the alcoholic's relapse also result in the family's relapse. So, keep the despair to a minimum, don't feed the alcoholic delusion that there is some trigger within the family for the relapse, and maintain your health and the health of the family instead of focusing all of your energy on the alcoholic.

You still have a life to live and a household to keep in order. You still have your mental health mechanisms in place and that is what will give the best opportunity for the alcoholic to once again choose recovery. The alcoholic will eventually tire of being the sickest person in the family and will want to show that he can contribute to the well being of the home. Until that happens, all you can do is pray for him and do the next right thing.

It will be difficult not to react to the alcoholic's insanity when he has been drinking. He may have spent the rent money and grocery money on booze. The children may be hungry. Your car may be out of gas, wrecked on in need of repair.

If the family has been taking care of themselves all along, going to Al-Anon and Alateen, or getting wise counsel from other people in similar circumstances, many of the negative consequences could have been avoided. While your alcoholic is still not trustworthy, which typically takes a year or more of sobriety, the family should have had preventive measures in place. Don't let the alcoholic fool you into believing he has done a complete turnaround unless there has been an incredible humbling before God. Lots of alcoholics are good at manipulating and selling themselves and others on the fact that they have changed. Many times they are only riding a temporary high and using their charm to get you on board.

The bank account, other financial resources, vehicles, and weapons should be protected from an alcoholic who has shown signs of dangerous conduct. If they have been arrested for driving while drunk, if they have broken up things in the house, if they have gambled away money or spent it on drunken sprees, or if they are having episodes of "blackouts" wherein they cannot recall what has happened, you are justified in getting help to protect the family.

These are things you will have heard from other families along the way and you should have some consensus among your family and support groups or therapists for implementing these safety measures. The alcoholic should have already heard your concerns and know that you are willing to do whatever is needed to protect the family from alcoholism. You may want to have that conversation with the alcoholic while accompanied by your own witnesses or support system. That conversation could also be part of an Orchestrated Intervention, but do not wait to arrange an intervention before laying the groundwork for protecting the family.

It is also not necessary to vocalize your emergency countermeasures. Part of your family safety may require secrecy among the healthy members in the family. You might want to keep a little emergency money and extra clothes in the car in case you need to make a quick getaway from an angry drunk. You may need to buy some life insurance on the alcoholic, with or without their permission. Again, the discussion about life insurance may be part of a broader intervention. Perhaps there are other things you will need to do to keep yourself or the family safe.

Sometime families react to alcoholic episodes in ways that are not productive. Bailing the alcoholic out of jail, searching the house for alcohol and pouring it out, paying his car payment, letting him live at home with his parents for free, nagging the alcoholic, calling and gossiping with the alcoholic's family or friends or A.A. sponsor, or calling work and making excuses for absences...these are all behaviors that will thwart sobriety rather than support it.

Even if you are careful not to light the fuse on the alcoholic time bomb, you are also in no position to try to halt the bomb from exploding. Don't try to manage the situation in an attempt to dampen the fuse because you are only delaying a bomb explosion. Wouldn't it be better just to quit playing around with the bomb? Simply put, it isn't your bomb to deactivate. Don't engage. Don't react. Don't tamper. Don't fix.

You can avoid making mistakes if you consult with an Al-Anon sponsor or other wise counsel before you make decisions. It is important your counsel have extensive experience instead of just opinions or a limited range of incidents they have heard about. This is no time for experimentation, guesswork, pop psychology, or encounters that emulate reality shows on TV.

Unfortunately, the alcoholic family is normally disoriented by a sudden and unexpected alcoholic crisis, thus the family is not often prepared to reason and seek sound advice before they react. Still other families are too embarrassed to seek wise counsel and feel they are exposing their family to public ridicule. Perhaps the family fears that the alcoholic might lose their job if exposed publicly. Even so, the family member must have wise counsel available even if they have memorized this book, are all prayed up, and think they don't need any help.

Before the alcoholic ever drinks again, you can help by engaging in some relapse prevention. The family shouldn't taunt the alcoholic or remind him of his past, they shouldn't keep alcohol within the home, nor give the alcoholic too much responsibility too soon. While you ultimately have no control over the alcoholic and his drinking, you need to also make sure you are not enabling the alcoholic's behavior.

Avoid being an alcoholic enabler! Don't buy them alcohol or give them money, but take care of their real world needs as best you can. Don't call work and report they are sick when they have a terrible hangover, but be willing to bring them the phone or help them get to a doctor. Don't let them drive the family car but give them a ride to legitimate meetings or help them on routine errands. If they have their own separate car and insist on driving, tell them that you will report them as a drunk driver should the need arise. Don't bail them out of jail, but don't prevent them from having access to money that is their own money.

Don't talk with them when they are sloppy drunk but be willing to have a conversation when they are lucid and able to communicate, realizing of course they may forget portions of it. Don't follow them around the house and talk to them, but maintain a presence in the home so that they can come to you and discuss issues. Don't abandon your home unless it is dangerous, but don't fuel arguments that help create the danger. Don't threaten divorce, but be willing to consult with spiritual counselors about how to proceed. Don't call the police because you are scared, call your spiritual mentors. Only call the police if violence has occurred or imminent. If they rip the phone out of the wall or take your cell phone, leave immediately. Then find a phone and call the police. If they can't help you, they will usually refer you to a resource. Hopefully, your own support system will be available.

Don't threaten to leave or order the alcoholic to leave, but be ready to take quick action should it become necessary. You should be able to leave quickly if need be and be willing to call the police if the alcoholic is no longer entitled to stay there. Most of all, don't position yourself as being the victim of the alcoholic, blaming the alcoholic for your difficulties, but also do not allow yourself to be victimized. If this all seems confusing, go to Al-Anon and talk to others.

If you or the dependent family is being victimized physically or financially, you must take immediate action and get somewhere safe and protect your assets. Run to a neighbor if need be and use their phone to call the police. If there is not imminent danger, but you are sensing an increased possibility of violence or financial ruin, you need to get wise counsel and make decisions as quickly as possible. If you are arguing with the alcoholic and trying to get them to understand, stop! The more you get your hands dirty, the more you desire to fix the situation, the more you obsess over the alcoholic's behavior, the more evidence exists that you are making yourself part of the problem.

That brings us to this. The most important piece of relapse prevention you can perform is on your own behalf. If you are making spiritual improvements in your life for the benefit of you and your family, then the alcoholic will also indirectly benefit. But you must be the primary person of concern. You must be healthy in order to be of any value to yourself or others. So, don't take any responsibility for the alcoholic and also don't do anything that will aggravate his condition.

Taking care of one's self is urgent. Consider a lesson from the airlines. After boarding an airplane and preparing for takeoff you receive instructions from the flight attendant as to how to survive a calamity in the air. This should be your lesson in taking care of yourself first. They ask you to put the oxygen mask on yourself before assisting anybody else. The point is simple. If you go unconscious you are of no use to others.

So it is with the alcoholic family. As the loved ones react imprudently in a crisis, as they fail to take care of their own needs appropriately, the family starts to suffer. They are like the person in the airplane that has been told to put on their oxygen mask first. Instead, the family might be mistakenly focusing all of their attention on the alcoholic, not realizing they are starving for oxygen in the process.

The alcoholic may be sitting in their own stupor, unaware of the crisis. They see the family make a great fuss over them and life in general. It doesn't impress the alcoholic because they are impaired.

The family thinks they are being heroic as they work on saving the alcoholic, but they fail to see they may be focusing so much on trying to save the alcoholic that the family may die of neglect. Many family members eventually tire of trying to save the alcoholic, but they have become so disillusioned in the process that the family has already suffered horribly. The unhealthy family will sometimes blame the alcoholic even though the family has created more damage by trying to help an uncooperative alcoholic.

The truth is that focusing on the alcoholic destroys the nonalcoholic. Even though the alcoholic is choosing to kill himself with liquor, the family is also dying from inattention. Strangely enough, the family can often survive by getting attention from the remaining healthy family members, but the health of the family suffers as they focus on the alcoholic and neglect their own well being.

On an airplane, if a fellow passenger is fighting you and keeps ripping off the oxygen mask you provide, you would at some point have to let them suffer the results. You can't allow their fighting to take down the entire plane. If they should die for lack of oxygen, better they die alone. So it is with the alcoholic that resists sobriety. It is better that they die alone than take the family with them.

That is a hard perspective to have but it works. It will also testify to the alcoholic that he is not the center of your universe. Coupled with the family's healthy faithfulness toward God, the alcoholic will continue to experience self conflict, preferably without the family adding to the drama. Eventually the alcoholic is emotionally isolated and sees the stark reality that he has nobody else to blame. Then they might find a way to humble themselves before God.

So how does the family deal with the ongoing and overwhelming frustration they experience as they wait for the alcoholic to get sober? The options are fight, flight or stand firm. Let's take some examples of how we might choose.

The alcoholic comes home drunk. Our initial instinct is disgust or anger. We are not really afraid of him and so we decide to give him a piece of our mind. We reason that he has it coming, that he will never change if he doesn't feel some pain. We are resentful of his cavalier approach, his lack of sensitivity to our concerns. We probably had been loading up on feelings and memories of similar past occurrences and we are willing and able to strike. How dare the alcoholic continue to flaunt his alcoholism in our face? How dare he continue to ignore the sanctity of our home?

Maybe we pick a fight by saying something sarcastic like, "I hope you had fun tonight." Or instead, perhaps we are earnest and request they sit down with us and talk. Or perhaps we give them the silent treatment and ignore the fact that they are even home. Perhaps we beg for attention. Maybe we are worried that they spent some desperately needed money and bring up something simple about the children needing lunch money, hoping to find out if there is any money left.

The unfortunate truth is that any of these things can set an alcoholic off on a tirade of anger. Even the silent treatment can be considered a way of picking a fight. We just cannot seem to win because the alcoholic is so uncaring and we can't seem to formulate a peaceful reaction.

So perhaps we don't fight and choose flight instead. We decide we will not be there when the alcoholic comes home. Maybe we go out drinking ourselves. We might go out of our way not to be there when the alcoholic comes home. Perhaps we have an extramarital affair or we move out. We file for a legal separation. We spend more time away from home than is good for the family. We may even be living out of suitcases and going to great lengths to avoid confrontations at home, convincing ourselves that we are doing our best.

The prospects of success by avoiding contact are not good. The family is not going to heal together if the members are apart. Still, some distance sometimes is necessary. Is there no safe middle ground where we are safe and stable? What do we do when we still haven't found the recipe for peace?

Therein lays the problem. We are trying to formulate our reaction to a problem that doesn't belong to us. We are trying to think of some way that we are going to feel okay about a very "not okay" situation. So we spend hours on end thinking about the alcoholic, how to help him get sober and how to keep ourselves safe and sane in the process. This is the typical dilemma of the alcoholic Christian family.

We are like passengers moving from deckchair to deckchair on the Titanic. We have this terrible sinking feeling that something bad is happening. We don't know what to do about it, so we start running to and fro and trying different things to see what will help. Well, we all know that switching deckchairs is not going to help. You may end up with a slightly different view of the tragedy, but it is still a tragedy.

Perhaps you start bailing water with a water glass. Again, we can engage in busy work, try to feel justified that we have tried everything in our power, but still nothing has changed. The boat is still sinking!

The only thing that will save the day is a change of course. Get some wise counsel. Perhaps a word with the Captain might help: "Dear Lord, what would you have me do in this set of circumstances? Please let me be a good steward of your blessings, and thank You for allowing me to serve my family. Amen"

Perhaps the Captain will tell you to steer the ship toward safe harbor. Perhaps he will tell you, for now, to quietly finish your dinner and wait. Perhaps he will tell you to prepare to abandon ship. Perhaps it is best if you still your mind and pray and wait on God to answer.

It is not going to be easy to still your mind in the middle of crisis, so it is wise to live in that stillness of the mind. Recall Romans 8:6 that that the mind controlled by the Spirit is life and peace. What we really need is to have peace, even in the midst of the storm. Indeed, especially in the midst of the storm!

You will recall we have proscribed deep spiritual work for the alcoholic. This is also true for the nonalcoholic. Just as the alcoholic has the genetic inheritance of a natural affinity for alcohol, the loved ones often have a natural affinity for the alcoholic. Also, just as the alcoholic must kick the alcohol habit by having a mind of peace, the loved one must kick the addiction to the alcoholic.

The family loves their alcoholic. They want him back. They focus all of their energy on him. They go to great efforts to save his life. Then they wake up one day and realize they don't have a life of their own. Somewhere along the way they became an appendage on the alcoholic, basing their well being upon their relationship with the alcoholic instead of their relationship with God.

Nobody quite knows when the relationship with the alcoholic took over, but the signs of defeat are there. It has become obvious to your deeply codependent soul that you too have become a wretch. A dry wretch, but a wretch all the same.

We have either hung on and fought it out, or ran in abandonment of hope. The results are the same. We accept defeat and the family has been destroyed. Like the alcoholic who is at the end of their rope, we are completely demoralized.

Also like the alcoholic, this can become the lowest rung of our ladder. If we will take this moment of clarity, this gift of demoralization, and realize that God has been trying to get our attention, we can start the climb up out of the mess.

We are now prepared to stand firm, not fighting imaginary enemies or running in fear. We no longer think of the alcoholic as our enemy and start to see him as a sick loved one. We realize this particular sickness can result in real worldly problems so we take prudent cautions to protect the family, but not out of resentment or retribution.

We are no longer trying to affect the alcoholic. We are simply taking care of our side of the street, keeping it clean and orderly. We are not caving in to the alcoholic in order to win favor, nor are we engaging in arguments. We are becoming a reasonable and calm person who is available to have a grownup conversation, but we are also willing to walk away from childish bickering.

We are busy living in the presence of God in our life. We have His peace and we will not let the tragedy of the alcoholic life ruin our relationship with God. Eventually, we will see that our mature, loving, and understanding nature disarms situations which use to spiral out of control.

We finally, like the alcoholic, must find God doing for us what we cannot do for ourselves. God is providing the very power to stay sober and sane. Let us bathe in the glory of God's grace, remembering that we are ultimately brothers and sisters in Christ even though we may also be husband and wife or parents and children.

It is no longer about power and control in our home because everybody acknowledges that God is the absolute leader in our home, that the father is meant to be a good spiritual leader therein, and that the mother or children may have to step into that role when the father is not available.

Life can become astonishingly simple when you put God first, yourself second, your family third, your job fourth, and the world fifth. People often argue that we should put our family or the world ahead of ourselves. This is good if we are being sacrificial, but you have to be completely healthy in order to be sacrificial and that means being true to yourself first so that you have the capacity to be sacrificial. It is true that there is an appropriate time to be a martyr, and it is okay to be a martyr, but only if God has called you to be a martyr. We are not allowed to make ourselves into a martyr and then expect to be glorified for that vain sacrifice.

When Jesus was martyred it was a request from the Father. Jesus submitted to the Father only. Recall that the devil asked Jesus to throw Himself off the highest point of the temple. Jesus refused to be tempted. Many of us are tempted to act self sacrificing because we think we should. "Should" is a dangerous word. It sets up expectations and expectations setup disappointments.

There is an old saying that is often sarcastically spoken regarding false martyrs, "Come down off the cross...we need the wood." In other words, your sacrifice is "your" sacrifice and is not from God. Quit pretending you are God's martyr. We have better things to do. By the way, this can apply for the alcoholic as well. Many an alcoholic has dramatically driven themselves to an alcoholic suicidal death because they were a false martyr feeling sorry for themselves and their horrible lot in life. They think that if only the world treated them better, they could get sober. Unfortunately, they would probably then choose to celebrate with a drink!

We all need to quit feeling sorry for ourselves. While the idle mind may be the devil's playground, self pity is the fertilizer in the devil's playground. Forget the alcoholic tragedy in your home and instead try to see the overall tragedy in the home that has nothing to do with alcohol. There are people suffering with no outlet and suffering will eventually end one way or another. Good or bad.

So, how do we stand firm without running or fighting? What does it mean to stand firm? If you haven't, read now Ephesians chapter 6 (NLT):

> [10] A final word: Be strong in the Lord and in his mighty power. [11] Put on all of God's armor so that you will be able to stand firm against all strategies of the devil. [12] For we are not fighting against flesh-and-blood enemies, but against evil rulers and authorities of the unseen world, against mighty powers in this dark world, and against evil spirits in the heavenly places.
>
> [13] Therefore, put on every piece of God's armor so you will be able to resist the enemy in the time of evil. Then after the battle you will still be standing firm. [14] Stand your ground, putting on the belt of truth and the body armor of God's righteousness. [15] For shoes, put on the peace that comes from the Good News so that you will be fully prepared. [16] In addition to all of these, hold up the shield of faith to stop the fiery arrows of the devil. [17] Put on salvation as your helmet, and take the sword of the Spirit, which is the word of God.
>
> [18] Pray in the Spirit at all times and on every occasion. Stay alert and be persistent in your prayers for all believers everywhere.

Be very aware that you have spiritual battles in your life. In these verses we are told to stand against evil three times. How do we stand? Firm! But what makes us able to stand firm? Read verse 13 (NLT) again: "Therefore, put on every piece of God's armor so you will be able to resist the enemy in the time of evil. Then after the battle you will still be standing firm."

You need every piece of the armor of God. Otherwise the weak spot in your armor will be the point of attack. Remember that you have three natural enemies as a Christian. They will be upon you for as long as you live, so putting on the whole armor of God daily will help you resist the temptations and attacks.

First, you have the flesh with its inherited weaknesses. Galatians 5 speaks clearly about the war between the Spirit of God within us and our very own flesh. We will need to train our mind, by the power of the Spirit of God within us, to resist the desires of the flesh. Each time we do so we grow stronger, more able to stand firm.

Even our very own feelings are flesh-based and subject to the influence of sin. In Ephesians 4:19 we see that we can become calloused and past the point of godly feelings when we live in sin. So as a people, we must test even our very own feelings against the word of God and seek good counsel from the spiritually mature brothers and sisters around us.

It is like a child learning to walk. Once you get the hang of it, you can do it without help, even without thinking. But it will take conscious effort to resist our strong feelings of the flesh, and those feelings and temptations become more subtle as we mature. The simple fact that we experience fewer repercussions as we spiritually mature can even lull us into complacency if we are not vigilant over the desires of our heart.

Secondly, the world is also our enemy, but not the people of the world. God loves the people enormously, but He hates what sin has done to corrupt His beloved and the perfect world He created. In 1 John 2:15 (NLT) we read, "Do not love this world nor the things it offers you, for when you love the world, you do not have the love of the Father in you."

We are not to love the "things" of this world. They are temporary. We have to be careful here. We can love the members of our family. We can even love the sanctity of the family that God has created. The family is the perfect example of godly unity upon the earth. But even so, we are not to put any of these godly ideals ahead of God. If you want proof, read the story of Abraham (Genesis 22) when he was asked to sacrifice his very own son. His son Isaac could hardly be considered a "thing," yet many of us put our alcoholics ahead of God, ahead of ourselves, or ahead of the family on a daily basis.

The point is that, if you are not careful, you may "love" the alcoholic to death. You may even enable him to his deathbed. There are many people who don't get sober until they are in their mid-forties because their parents have continued to take care of them long after they should have forced the child to grow up. When the family does this it is not love. It is enabling behavior and the sin now rests also with the parents, not just with the aging wayward child.

Here is a case where a parent's godly love is not accompanied by godly discipline. Since the child is now grown they don't think it right to discipline them now. Realizing it is too late to raise the child properly they settle on enabling the child as they hope the child finally quits drinking. The parents need Al-Anon. There they will learn they have been easing their conscience by enabling the alcoholic behavior of their child. They don't mean to kill the child with kindness, they just don't know what else to do and they often don't understand. Simply put, they have never allowed the child to fail miserably and they need to start as soon as possible. They might also apologize to the alcoholic child for the delayed parenting. Truly, it is easier for a young child to learn the lesson of failure than it is for a forty year old.

This is why it is important for every family to engage with outside sources for emotional support. It may take some people an extraordinary amount of time to finally understand how to handle their situation in a godly way, while others will benefit quickly and start sharing their experiences as they find a still greater peace by being of service to others. Young and old, inexperienced or veterans, everybody wins who participates in God's work of saving people and families.

Even in our very own house, the healthy attitude can move from person to person. One day Farris is struggling, the next day he is our fortress. One day Ruth feels defeated, another day she is our source of endless encouragement. In turn, families within your fellowship community will be able to alternatively help each other from time to time. Farris has a saying among the men of his ministry, "The reason the fellowship works is because they are not all insane on the same day." So, don't be afraid to share your difficulties with others and accept their encouragement, nor should you feel unqualified to offer support, even to the strongest among us. This is how the body of Christ functions and empowers us to survive the ways of the world.

Our third enemy is evil itself. We discussed in depth the role of evil in alcoholism, but evil is equally cunning within the life of a nonalcoholic. The nonalcoholic naturally assumes they are the victim and cannot see how they have done anything wrong. They don't realize they are wrongly fighting evil when they confront the alcoholic. It is not our job to fight that evil. It is our job to support the alcoholic in getting sober so that the alcoholic can then wrestle against the evil that attacks them.

We should instead hold the alcoholic at a safe distance. We don't engage them at all unless they are in a condition to safely communicate. We should not think we are being sacrificial by engaging the alcoholic graciously unless the alcoholic is able to also be civilized with us.

Sometimes the alcoholic may bring evil to us by accusing us of being selfish or prudish. Drunken husbands have been known to accuse their wives of being frigid because the wife didn't want to have romance with the drunken alcoholic. The alcoholic evil might then come loudly, trying to control the nonalcoholic with bully tactics, wanting to make the nonalcoholic feel guilty. The nonalcoholic should strive to calmly say that you respect yourself enough to not compromise your morals. Perhaps you can invite the alcoholic to enjoy a sober night of fun with you and really mean it.

We will never know for sure how evil is coming after us. We will not see demons or devils heading our way. Instead we see confused people, or manipulators, or drunks. So, rather than worry about what is being driven by evil, it is simply better to live a principled and intentional existence.

We don't have to judge the world; we only have to maintain our sanctity within the world. If we are careful about each move, if we let God direct our thoughts and next right actions, we are sure to become better able to live in peace. That is the hope we can bring to the table and this is how we can begin to see horrible situations change.

So, how do we make it to the Promised Land where milk and honey flow? The answer is a question, "What kept the children of Israel from making it to Canaan? Why did it take forty years for them to make a trip that should have never taken more than a couple of months, even with the old folks and baggage and animals?" After all, it was only about 250 miles if they had not taken the long road home.

That is the point, the long road home. As we look at their long road to the Promised Land, let us each be aware of our own long road home.

We find that God used the exodus as a way to teach the Israelites. In Deuteronomy 8 (NLT) we read:

> "Be careful to obey all the commands I am giving you today. Then you will live and multiply, and you will enter and occupy the land the LORD swore to give your ancestors. Remember how the LORD your God led you through the wilderness for these forty years, humbling you and testing you to prove your character, and to find out whether or not you would obey his commands. Yes, he humbled you by letting you go hungry and then feeding you with manna, a food previously unknown to you and your ancestors. He did it to teach you that people do not live by bread alone; rather, we live by every word that comes from the mouth of the LORD. For all these forty years your clothes didn't wear out, and your feet

didn't blister or swell. Think about it: Just as a parent disciplines a child, the LORD your God disciplines you for your own good.

"So obey the commands of the LORD your God by walking in his ways and fearing him. For the LORD your God is bringing you into a good land of flowing streams and pools of water, with fountains and springs that gush out in the valleys and hills. It is a land of wheat and barley; of grapevines, fig trees, and pomegranates; of olive oil and honey. It is a land where food is plentiful and nothing is lacking."

So, we are being commanded, tested and proven by the Lord. With the kind of power He has, it is important that we pay attention, don't you think? It isn't punishment He metes out. God is disciplining us for *our* own good, not His. If we will only believe and trust, we will inherit the land of plenty from Him.

You know what it is to believe. Now we want you to act in trust. Recall that faith without works is dead? Now, take the resources you have been given, gather the trusted loved ones around you and prepare for a new life. Be patient and be slow to anger. You may be the person who saves your family. May God bless your every effort!

I will do something.
I will do something with this information.
I will do something with this information soon.
I will do something with this information real soon.

Spiritual Tools for Your Toolkit

Depend on God

Self-sufficiency is in our blood, our heritage, and our ancestry. We are taught to "pull ourselves up by our bootstraps." Modern self-help books tell us to find the answers within ourselves. We feel sorry for the handicapped and aged, because they are clearly dependent on others. We may feel superior to our loved one, who seems to depend on us. We are proud of our strength and get-'er-done spirit.

Even "God helps those who help themselves," says Benjamin Franklin. Imagine our dismay when we discover that we can't do everything on our own. Asking for help becomes a confession of weakness. We feel judged by a culture that idolizes independence and competence.

Our self-sufficiency suppresses our needs, but does not remove them, as evidenced by our worry and pain. God invites us to bravely expose all our needs to Him (Philippians 4:19). Nothing is too trivial (Isaiah 65:24). Dependence is relying on someone; independence is relying on no one; interdependence is a dynamic of being mutually and physically responsible for each other. Independence is a leftover survival tool fueled by overactive pride.

Sanity will return to us if we learn dependence on God (Acts 17:25), interdependence with our loved one (Titus 3:14), and prayer that our loved one will also find peace through dependence on God (Romans 1:9).

Well, do you want My help or not?

Do the Right Thing, Not the Easy Thing

Living with unreasonable people is not easy. Some of our friends will tell us that it's so much easier to live on our own, make our own decisions, keep to our own schedule, and even watch whatever we want on television. If our home is peaceful and relaxed, then easy is good, right?

French philosopher Voltaire said, "The better is the enemy of good." The wisdom that God wants for us cannot be found along the smooth path to an easier lifestyle. We settle for easy by sacrificing spiritual maturity. Although it's a cliché, we should realize that our experiences build our character as well as generate a testimony that is an asset in God's Kingdom. The purpose of our struggles, however, is not to enable our loved ones to wallow in a carefree lifestyle.

In 2 Corinthians 8:13 (NLT), Paul says, "Of course, I don't mean your giving should make life easy for others and hard for yourselves. I only mean that there should be some equality." We should heed the advice of Bishop Phillips Brooks: "Do not pray for easy lives. Pray to be stronger men. Do not pray for tasks equal to your powers. Pray for powers equal to your tasks. Then the doing of your work shall be no miracle, but you shall be the miracle."

We should renounce easy, remembering that in this boot camp called Earth, the more prepared we are, the better off we will be as we continue our journey in fellowship with God.

Try Something Different

Practice makes perfect, and many of us are motivated to practice and practice conversing with our loved ones. We want to get better at it, so we schedule family meetings and heart-to-heart talks and interventions. But like an incorrect golf swing, the only thing more communication practice gives us is complete knowledge of how to do it the wrong way. We develop bad habits.

Albert Einstein's definition of insanity is "doing the same thing over and over again and expecting different results." We generally don't try new behaviors because we risk losing face if the outcome isn't as expected or we fear losing someone's approval. The worst part is that we feel like such wimps to be so caught up in our fears that we cannot communicate effectively with our loved ones at all.

George S. Patton said, "Take calculated risks. That is quite different from being rash." So, we should not rush headlong to try out any new idea that pops into our heads, but we should experiment cautiously. We should try new words, new quiet times, new ideas, new actions, and new inactions, all for the purpose of building our character.

We should have no expectations that the new behaviors will result in getting our loved one to respond. Indeed, many new behaviors may feel like failures. However, as Thomas A. Edison remarked, "I have not failed. I've just found 10,000 ways that won't work." New behaviors are scary and there's a lot at stake. The concept "do not fear" appears in the Bible 365 times, admonishing us daily to not fear life, but to honor God.

**If you want something different,
DO something different.**

See People through God's Eye

Due to our caring nature, we spend many hours reviewing the faults of our loved ones in order to help them become better people. We reason that if our companions improve their lives, then our lives would improve as well, alleviating some of our pain and suffering.

It comes as a surprise, therefore, to find out that our suffering is not related to our loved one's lifestyle at all. God tells us in Jeremiah 31:30 that each of us suffers for our own sin, not for another's. If we want to stop suffering, we must appeal to God for improvement of self rather than progress for someone else.

Finding fault in another is easily learned. We may have learned it from our loved ones, who have obviously spent time identifying and criticizing our character. However, we don't become better people by identifying someone else's problems. Self-criticism won't help us either, as that usually results in self-pity. If we want to see the problem, we need to look at ourselves and our loved ones through God's forgiving eyes rather than our own critical eyes. Here our caring nature will be a great asset, because it is in seeing ourselves and our loved ones as God sees us that we find honest solutions. God is not looking for perfection but for "constant improvement" (Revelation 2:19).

Extend Courtesy

We tend to like people who are similar to ourselves. Close quarters with another person highlights our dissimilarities. Familiarity really does breed contempt, as well as disrespect and disinterest. Even characteristics we once treasured in our loved ones become irritating.

The longer we look deep into our loved one's psyche, the less we find there to respect. However, there is good news. Respect is learned, not innate, behavior. In Titus 4:2, Paul tells us that older women teach the younger women respect. If respect is learned behavior, then we should no longer be concerned about whether or not our loved one earns our respect. Instead, we can focus on learning the discipline of respect.

Unfortunately, many materials misdirect us into thinking that we must learn to respect ourselves before learning to respect others. We'll find nothing in the Bible, however, about respecting ourselves before others. What we find instead is instruction on learning respectful behavior. We'll find courtesy, like bowing in Genesis 18:2, and standing in Job 29:8, and warm gestures in Acts 27:3, and kind receiving in Acts 28:7. We'll find commands to speak courteously in Colossians 4:6 and to be kind in Ephesians 4:32.

We should start learning respect with baby steps. If our loved one is a spouse or parent, we may think about the respect we have for other spouses and parents due to the challenges and difficulty of the position. We may consider God's sovereignty in putting our loved one into relationship with us.

Perhaps God did not intend for our loved one to do a good job in the position of spouse or parent yet, but intends for our encouragement to boost our loved one's abilities. Regardless of our understanding or feelings, however, God commands us to act courteously (Romans 12:10).

Peter tells us that even the undeserving master is shown respect (1 Peter 2:18). It is through the method of becoming respectful people that God gifts us with prized possessions: self-respect (Proverbs 11:16), the respect of others (Proverbs 13:15), and something to respect in our loved one (Daniel 1:9).

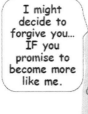

Fresh Start

A Fresh Start sounds great! A New Beginning calls to our sense of adventure. Leave all that damage behind, and start a new _____. Fill in the blank: New job. New relationship. New home. New friends. New life. We're thinking that anything's got to be better than our current situation. Our culture concurs: the grass is greener on the other side of the fence. We're so far down, the only way to go is up.

Within 12-step programs, this action is called a geographic cure. We opt for a quick fix based on two lies: 1) that our current situation is unfixable and 2) that change is always for the better.

In The Imitation of Christ, Thomas à Kempis reveals the truth, "So, the cross is always ready and waits for you everywhere. You cannot escape it no matter where you run, for wherever you go you are burdened with yourself. Wherever you go, there you are."

Because we bring our character defects with us wherever we go, we will reinsert the same problems and concerns that currently plague us into any new situation. Change cannot be pushed into our lives from the outside. Rather, change starts in our hearts (Deuteronomy 10:16) and overflows to our lives.

Our "Fresh Start" tool includes two assurances. The first is that God is all about doing for us what we cannot do for ourselves, including the mending of an unfixable situation. The second is that if we're looking for a change for the better, we need go no further than down to our knees in prayer, for "Whatever is good and perfect comes down to us from God our Father, who created all the lights in the heavens" (James 1:17, NLT). We should do our part by staying put in our situation so that God can change our hearts (2 Timothy 2:25). Or, as the 12-step programs say, "Don't leave before the miracle happens."

Forgiveness

Many Christians mistakenly think that God has forgotten our sins. Simply put, He sees our sins but forgives them in honor of His Son, Jesus Christ. The sins of believers are covered by the blood sacrifice of Jesus and it is His resurrection victory that empowers us to forgive others and eliminate sin from being dominant in our lives.

None of us deserve forgiveness, and forgiveness cannot be earned no more than a wrong can be undone. The wrongs of life live in space and time and can be ignored and forgiven, but the actions are not erased from history. Jesus asked the Father to forgive the people "for they know not what they do." Yet, the history of their sinful actions live on in the Bible even though they were forgiven by the Master Himself.

Still, in Colossians 3:13 we are instructed, "Make allowance for each other's faults, and forgive anyone who offends you. Remember, the Lord forgave you, so you must forgive others" (NLT).

So, we make allowances for the imperfections of the people around us. In Luke 6:37, Jesus tells us, "Do not judge others, and you will not be judged. Do not condemn others, or it will all come back against you. Forgive others, and you will be forgiven" (NLT).

So, how can we forgive somebody over and over if they seem to continue the same wrongful acts? In Matthew 18:21-22 (NLT) we read, "Then Peter came to him and asked, 'Lord, how often should I forgive someone who sins against me? Seven times?' 'No, not seven times,' Jesus replied, 'but seventy times seven!'" Jesus makes the simple point that we should continuously forgive regardless of our feelings.

Corrie Ten Boom said, "Forgiveness is an act of the will, and the will can function regardless of the temperature of the heart." We must remember that our heart may not always feel the forgiveness we have given, but once we have forgiven, we have no right to revoke it. That right has been forfeited and we can no longer hold the person accountable for that wrong.

If they continue to sin we can hold them accountable for the new sins, we don't set aside their worldly consequences and enable their bad behavior by our forgiveness, but we must avoid bringing up the past sins that have been forgiven.

We must not allow temptation to overcome us. We may want to say, "You'll never change" but instead need to say, "I know how hard it is to change. Let's talk about what we can do." You may want to say, "You always mess things up" but instead need to say, "I'm here to help you when you're ready."

Remember, they have already been forgiven for the past and we have no right to bring it up again. Indeed, we must, in prayer and humility, instead prepare to forgive the new sins against us. So while we don't condemn them, we can still find it wise to hold them accountable. We don't comment on their character or personality flaws. When the time is right we instead comment on their actions. They are not living a trust-worthy life, so we can't trust them in certain things, but we don't cast blame or pass moral judgment. We protect ourselves and our family and move forward.

The ultimate point of forgiveness is simple. Pray for forgiveness, agree to not hold a lingering resentment about the past, and pray for God to remove the poisonous anger of blame. Despite any additional sinful behavior by others, the person who has prayed and forgiven others has received peace as a benefit of the forgiveness they gave.

If you find yourself getting angry and starting to have hard feel-ings again about the situation, you haven't taken back your forgiveness, you simply have something new to pray about. Most Christians have to pray often to reinforce the godly decisions they have made that might later be denied by their fleshly heart.

Get out of God's Way

Our loved one may be angry, but not at us. He or she may direct the anger at us, and even try to blame us for the anger, but only our loved one owns the anger. This anger will spill out onto whoever or whatever happens to be handy, usually us, the family members.

Our "Get out of God's Way" tool requires four levels of detachment. First, we detach physically. We have prepared a safe place in our home, perhaps a prayer closet, corner of our kitchen, or even the laundry room, where we can regroup with others that are affected. Our children need reassurance as much as we do, so we should invite them into our safe place.

Second, we detach mentally. We remember that it is our loved ones' anger, not ours. We should not focus on the cause or containment of the rage. Instead, we direct our attention to whatever task we would normally be doing if the rage were not at hand.

Third, we detach emotionally. We are not required to feel fear, nor are we required to redirect the anger, since it doesn't belong to us. We should take personal inventory and verify that we feel only our emotions and not emotions that overflow from our loved one.

Finally, we detach spiritually. God does not take sides. Our loved one's anger and our depression are both urgent in God's eyes. The messy words spilling out of our loved one's mouth and the messy thoughts swirling around in our heads are equally harmful. We plead to God, as Jesus prayed, not to "take [us] out of the world, but to keep [us] safe from the evil one" (John 17:15). We realize we have detached spiritually when we can pray for our angry loved one using the same words we use when we pray for our own safety and the safety of our children.

I'm practicing how to detach with love... I figured I better start with something easy.

Working Alongside God

God has equipped us with a helping heart. This precious gift is ours to provide to a desperate world: to be a helper extraordinaire, to assist where others give up, and to pour all our enthusiasm and work ethic into being the hands and feet of our Savior while we're here. We help and help, and we especially help our loved ones. But sometimes the end result is that our family members are burning with resentment and we feel unappreciated. What happened?

Chicken farmers know that the more help a hatchling receives breaking out of its shell, the more likely the chicken will die once outside its shell. The hatchlings require the long, painfully slow struggle out of their egg in order to emerge strong enough to survive in the world. The struggle is intentional by God's design.

In the Old Testament, God purposely leaves pagan nations in Canaan (Judges 3:1). We watch the Israelites struggle against these nations in order to "teach warfare to generations of Israelites who had no experience in battle" (Judges 3:2). By the same token, God provides struggles for our loved ones so that they will emerge strong enough to thrive in a broken world. When we stop assisting our loved ones, it may seem to us as though we are standing by helplessly as we watch them struggle. This is not the case.

The blessing of our helping heart is to learn to assist in the way God would have us, instead of the more obvious worldly help that we're used to giving. Although we should not assist with our loved ones' outward struggles, we should intercede regularly through prayer and meditation, asking God to show us how to help His way.

It looks like his struggles
are paying off.

I'm Sorry You Feel That Way

We seem to lose many arguments with our loved ones. We feel that we're not as eloquent, or maybe that our loved ones are somehow holding all the cards and fixing the conflict in their favor. Regardless, we walk away from many an argument feeling defeated.

Perhaps our loved ones attack our character. We intuitively know that's not fair. We can label it hurtful, or hateful, or abusive, but none of that will make anybody feel better, communicate better, or resolve the situation better. When someone resorts to character assassination, the communication is clear: they feel like they have not been heard.

Our job (gulp) is to listen. Compounding the difficulty, however, is our belief that arguments are a contest in which there's a winner and a loser. We should understand that our manipulative loved ones will be much better at unreasonable arguments than we are. They are more practiced and better prepared to spin facts, skew logic, and blindside their opponent.

Our "I'm sorry you feel that way" tool is actually two tools wrapped in one. The first is visualization. When we are being verbally abused, we might pretend that we're a duck, and the words being thrown at us are drops of water, calmly dripping back into the pond. Just because someone is saying something does not make it true, and listening doesn't mean agreeing.

The second aspect of our "I'm sorry you feel that way" tool is non-retaliation. If we didn't listen to our loved one, then we have no right to expect that they are going to listen to us. If we even suspected they cared, we certainly would have attacked our loved ones, if we could have gotten a word in edgewise.

In any event, we should become willing to disengage from any and all unreasonable conflicts. During the conflict, when our loved ones pause after a particularly hurtful remark, our response is "I'm sorry you feel that way." And we are truly sorry that our loved ones hurt to the point of feeling the need to attack us.

I don't know if I will ever be able to say "I'm sorry you feel that way." My mouth seems to have other words in mind!

Speak Carefully

"Do not let any unwholesome talk come out of your mouths, but only what is helpful for building others up according to their needs, that it may benefit those who listen" (Ephesians 4:29, NIV). Our alcoholic loved one doesn't seem to be in need, though, when he or she arrives home drunk, disorderly, late, and "partied out". A tongue lashing seems more in order.

That's why 12-step groups often refer to the nonalcoholic loved one as the "mouth-at-the-door." It's as if our voice-on button is attached to the doorknob, so that as soon as our loved one enters, we start in with where-have-you-been, who-were-you-with, what-were-you-doing, what-were-you-thinking, and how-could-you-do-this-to-me.

What we fail to see is the tortured, angry, incoherent soul hiding behind the false bravado of a party animal. What we fail to see is our caring and compassionate heart hiding underneath our irritated and irrational barrage of words. Our intention is to correct our loved one's behavior, but instead the frustration and anger bubbles over into a harsh exchange.

Communication requires both a speaker and a listener. Even though our words speak the truth, our audience is not available to hear them. Thomas Jefferson said it best: "When angry, count ten before you speak; if very angry, a hundred."

We should remember that our enemy isn't the lost person standing in front of us; it's the great liar that stands in our loved one's stead. That's why we should plead with God to rescue us from the evil one (Matthew 6:13) and hold our tongues. We should honor our commitment to bring the truth to the attention of our loved ones by delaying our interchange until a better time.

How am I going to handle this?
What do I Say? What do I do?

Keep the Peace

We've reached a breaking point, so we let our loved one know, in no uncertain terms, exactly how we feel. No holds barred, we let it all out. Our culture treats discontent like food poisoning that we need to get out of our system by yelling and lashing out. We repeat over and over again the standards that our family members seem to be ignoring.

When we realize they're obviously not listening, we up the ante by adding the guaranteed-to-get-their-attention word daggers: the words 'always' and 'never'. Laurence J. Peter, best known for the tongue-in-cheek Peter Principle, said, "Speak when you are angry--and you will make the best speech you'll ever regret."

We get nothing out of our system by lashing out. Instead, the momentary power surge of anger fuels our unhappiness, teaching us to repeat our temper tantrums whenever we feel frustrated. Our "Keep the Peace" tool does not mean that we do not have the right to speak. It means that we do not have the right to speak in anger.

Quarrels are not won by volume or by repetition. If we really want the attention of our family members, we should start with earnest petition to God to mold our hearts in preparation for serious business with our loved ones. Then we gently speak (1 Timothy 5:1-2 and Proverbs 15:1).

When I said we should learn to live in peace, I really didn't plan on smoking a peace pipe with you!

Kindness

Kindness is such a tricky thing. We want to be kind, and God tells us to be kind (Proverbs 11:17), and we have the gift of kindness (Romans 12:8). Why is it, then, that as hard as we try to be kind, our actions are misunderstood and unappreciated? We act kindly only to feel exploited and misused when we give an inch and our loved one takes a mile.

We spend time reviewing all the unkindnesses of our loved ones to God. Do we think God somehow missed those transgressions? This is called whining. Perhaps we spend time with our loved one reviewing the list of their unkindnesses. This is called nagging. We spend time reviewing all the unkindnesses of our loved one to others. This is called gossip. We spend time reviewing all the unkindnesses of our loved ones to ourselves. This is called judgment.

The poet Kahlil Gibran said, "I have learned silence from the talkative, tolerance from the intolerant and kindness from the unkind. I should not be ungrateful to those teachers."

Perhaps God provides us with teachers of unkindness so that we can reach a more practical level of kindness in our lives. Our serenity depends on our ability to intertwine our compassionate heart with self-control. Our environment contains both lessons on practical kindness as well as someone on which to practice kindness. We should pray for God's guidance in how to demonstrate healthy concern for our loved one, and in doing so, provide our family members with an example of kindness.

Kevin is having trouble with his new mentor on the Christian Academy Football team.

Not Broken

When our relationships are stormy, we suffer heartbreaking indecision. What do we do when we can't feel love and the bonds are clearly broken? Our indecision occurs because we find no use for thankless relationships.

We throw all broken items away whether they are malfunctioning vacuum cleaners or dysfunctional attachments to people. God, on the other hand, only uses things that are first allowed to be broken: broken hearts (Psalm 34:18), broken spirits (Psalm 51:17), broken bodies (1 Corinthians 15:43), broken defenses (Psalm 60:1), broken emotions (Psalm 51:8), all for the purpose of being restored by our Creator.

Leon Morris, the Australian New Testament scholar, said, "When the high seas are raging, it's no time to change ships." We should consider the possibility that God needs to rework our current relationships with our loved ones in order to resurrect those bonds into something meaningful and useful. This might well be the time to batten down the hatches, lower the sails, and ride out the storm in the safety of God's ship rather than face the onslaught in our own small rowboat.

"Put on some lotion, Henry, the sun is our worst enemy."

Pain is Only a Memory

Regardless of whether or not we remember the issue from our last argument, we certainly remember the fallout: what we said, what we did, and the pain of watching our loves ones retaliate or retreat. Even if the issue was important and the outcome was tolerable, we still have residual pain which will spill over into the very next conflict.

Therein lays the key. The only place the pain exists is in our memory. Whether the conflict was ten minutes ago or ten years ago, it's not happening right now. We have a choice as to what to store in memory. God commands us to remember His name (Exodus 3:15), His laws (Exodus 12:24), His covenant (Jeremiah 11:6), and His works (Isaiah 46:9). God commands us to remember mistakes so that we can do better next time. But there's no commandment to relive the pain of a quarrel over and over.

Author Sir James M. Barrie said, "God gave us memory that we might have roses in December." God has designed our memory to be used for the purposes of learning and improving. If the pain doesn't help with that, we should appeal to God to overcome our addiction to misery.

"Why are Bob's ideas always called 'concepts',
while mine are called 'notions'?"

**Stanley thought of himself as a victim.
He remembered every time he was offended.**

You May be Right

Lady Dorothy Fanny Nevill said, "The real art of conversation is not only to say the right thing at the right place but to leave unsaid the wrong thing at the tempting moment." The Bible concurs, commanding us to be "quick to listen, slow to speak, and slow to get angry" (James 1:19, NLT).

In the midst of a confrontation, we are so eager to make our point that we rarely consider, or even listen, to our loved one's point of view. Perhaps the heated dialogue is moving quickly and we feel the need to defend our points and prepare counterpoints.

Regardless, our path to spiritual growth requires us not only to monitor our tongue, but also to open our mind to our loved one's concerns. Even before we completely understand the full meaning of what our loved one is saying, we have the opportunity to reply, "You may be right."

Fortunately, this does not mean that our loved one is right and that we are wrong. It doesn't even mean that there is a right and a wrong. It means that we don't yet know who, if anyone is right and that we're willing to weigh all the alternatives. In Matthew 7:3 (NLT), Jesus asks us, "And why worry about a speck in your friend's eye when you have a log in your own?" Perhaps both we and our family members have logs in our eyes, but we should pray that God allow us to consider all the possibilities.

Reminders

1. Change begins with me.

2. We cannot fix anybody, even ourselves. We can only humble ourselves before God and ask for the strength to resist temptation.

3. Alcoholism and addictions affect the whole family.

4. You are not alone. Find other people that share your difficulties. Church and 12-step programs are good places to start.

5. You are a spiritual being having a human experience. Focus on spirit more and more and quit making human excuses.

6. Everybody is addicted to something. It is the way of the flesh.

7. Don't get too excited over progress, or too discouraged over setbacks.

8. The goal for the family should be to live a successful, fruitful life whether the alcoholic is sober or not.

9. Live with an attitude of gratitude. It is more important to want what you have than it is to get what you want.

10. Don't be proud of what you have accomplished, be grateful for what God has done through you.

11. Experience is what you get when you don't get what you want.

12. Forgive but don't forget. Then pray and forgive again.

13. Forgive, but don't forget. Only remind people when God really needs you to remind them.

14. Change starts with you and soon finds fertile soil in others. Be patient.

15. Praise loudly and criticize quietly.

16. Explain your anger instead of showing it.

17. There is nothing so horrible that a drink can't make it worse.

18. Alcoholism is suicide on the installment plan.

19. Notice the gifts and talents of others...we are all unique creations.

20. If alcohol is the solution, alcoholism is the problem.

21. "First you take a drink, then the drink takes a drink, then the drink takes you." -F. Scott Fitzgerald

22. If you are at your last straw, call the hospital, 911, or state mental health agency. Get a referral.

23. Alcohol affects people differently at different times.

24. You can only live one day at a time.

25. Always give people a chance to make amends, but that doesn't mean you give them another chance to take advantage of you.

26. Good judgment comes from experience, and experience comes from bad judgment.

27. To have more in life, just desire less.

28. Having a resentment toward others is like drinking poison and hoping someone else dies. Express your anger appropriately.

29. People don't care how much you know until they know how much you care.

30. If you don't know what's appropriate, ask for sage advice.

31. This too shall pass.

32. Search your heart each night for things that have offended God and man.

33. You have one mouth and two ears. Use them that way.

34. Work a process to reduce your character defects and their effects on others.

35. We are disconnected from God and counterfeit comforts won't fix that problem. We need God.

36. Serenity is not the absence of conflict. It is peace despite the conflict.

37. Don't just go to the altar, live at the altar.

38. Eternity is set within your heart.

39. We all have too big an appetite for something...pray for God to take over your appetite.

40. Feelings are not facts.

41. Romance is God's way of getting the right people together. Commitment is what keeps us together.

42. I'm sorry you feel that way.

43. Romance novels create fantasies and unrealistic expectations, just like pornography.

44. The flesh is a cruel master.

45. Ask yourself any time you want, "Am I being selfish or sacrificial?"

46. Go to the Comforter rather than what comforts you.

47. Just for Today; is God your pilot, copilot, or passenger?

48. It is good to have grown up adult conversations if you can.

49. Once you are delivered, do what it takes to stay delivered.

50. There is no high like the Most High

51. You have three natural enemies: the flesh, the world, and evil.

52. Sometimes doing nothing is the most you can do.

53. Put on the armor of God daily (read Ephesians 6).

54. Get your priorities right each day; take care of yourself as a sacrifice to others.

55. Love without discipline is permissiveness and will "love them to death."

56. Discipline without love is cruelty and not to be trusted.

57. Pray first, out loud if possible, then meditate and listen for God to speak to your heart.

58. "No" is a complete sentence. Stand firm in it as needed.

59. God is doing for us what we cannot do for ourselves.

60. Don't leave before the miracle happens.

61. You may be right

62. How to Communicate

    a.   Pray first

    b.   Identify the posture of the people

    c.   Listen twice and speak once

    d.   Confirm what you think you heard

    e.   Confess your weaknesses, not theirs

    f.   Be brave and honest

    g.   Remain calm and unaggressive

    h.   Leave with things learned

No need to feel alone.

"Yeah, I hate change, too."

YOUR NEXT STEPS

The Authors, Chaplain Farris and Ruth Robertson, can be reached through Recovery Literature, 217 W. Bennett St. Springfield, Missouri 65807. They make themselves available to lead conferences, mentor organizations, and provide spiritual counsel as time may allow. Let us know if you have the ability to host a conference and we will help all we can. We will look forward to hearing from you, and you can always visit our website at www.RecoveryLiterature.com.

There are a variety of Christian Ministries that work with alcoholics or addicts. There are not so many available for the families. That is why the Authors are hoping to see families arise from among God's people and embrace Al-Anon while they also establish a separate *Christian Family Recovery* group in their locale. Recovery Literature is dedicated to providing the resources necessary to facilitate ministries where family members can learn and practice together.

Meanwhile, there are already existing meetings for alcoholics, addicts, and family members all over the world. The most abundant meetings are 12-step meetings and can be found through local phone books or internet searches. Christian meetings for recovering addicts and alcoholics are quite plentiful. Some are general Christian Ministries for a wide array of suffering people.

Whether you are brand new to 12-step programs or church, whether you have backslid or not, you are likely to experience anxiety about going into a new and strange meeting environment. This is a critical juncture. You own mind will make excuses and tell you that it won't work for your situation. Your feelings of being overwhelmed in life will also make it difficult to commit effort and resources to engaging is a process with whcih you are not familiar or comfortable.

It is urgent that you overcome (Revelation 3:21) your concerns and attend a meeting several times before you judge its value for your life. If that meeting, after six visits, isn't working for you, then you must try another meeting location for six visits. God will surely honor your devotion and lead you to a home group that is right for you.

When choosing what groups to attend, try to locate people or families in similar situations to your own. Being careful and aware in unfamiliar meeting environments will help you feel safe as you explore. Always associate with the people who are serious about their individual recovery. The world of addictions is full of disorders and selfish manipulations, and people in recovery can readily slip back into old behaviors, even if they are clean and sober. Help God put integrity into every aspect of recovery. After all, we are His body upon the earth.

Be of service to others as soon as you are able. Bring your share of God's light into a world that has been darkened by self-centeredness. Your work in His behalf will increase your peace of mind. Feelings of being useful to God will overcome feelings of hopelessness. You will likely exhibit newly found patience with those around you. This is the beauty of change. The courage that started with you and can now find fertile soil in others.

Index

abandonment 115, 126
Abraham 129
abstinence 61, 63
acceptance 5, 42
accountability 68
accountable 83, 139, 140
acknowledgment 55
addiction 5, 6, 10, 14, 19, 20, 21, 22, 126, 148
addicts 21, 68, 79, 155
affection 20, 32, 34, 52
affectionate 34
affections 25
affliction 6, 62, 99
aggressive 34
aggressiveness 55
al-anon 32, 82, 98, 102, 112, 116, 121, 122, 123, 130, 155
alcohol 5, 13, 14, 15, 16, 17, 20, 21, 22, 23, 24, 25, 32, 33, 42, 63,
64, 65, 66, 69, 70, 71, 72, 73, 74, 77, 78, 98, 100, 106, 109, 113,
119, 120, 122, 126, 128, 152, 155
alcohol-is-m 99
alcohol-was-m 99
alcoholic 6, 9, 10, 11, 14, 15, 16, 17, 20, 21, 22, 24, 25, 26, 29, 30,
31, 32, 33, 34, 35, 39, 48, 52, 53, 61, 62, 63, 64, 65, 66, 67, 69, 70,
71, 72, 78, 79, 80, 81, 82, 83, 87, 89, 92, 93, 94, 97, 98, 99, 100,
101, 102, 103, 104, 105, 106, 109, 110, 111, 112, 113, 114, 115,
116, 117, 119, 120, 121, 122, 123, 124, 125, 126, 127, 128, 130,
131, 144, 151

alcoholics 5, 10, 16, 20, 21, 23, 24, 31, 48, 61, 62, 63, 65, 66, 67, 68, 69, 70, 71, 72, 79, 80, 82, 91, 95, 97, 99, 100, 101, 102, 109, 112, 113, 117, 121, 129, 155

alcoholism 5, 6, 21, 22, 24, 25, 27, 29, 30, 31, 32, 33, 35, 39, 61, 62, 63, 64, 65, 66, 69, 70, 71, 72, 77, 81, 82, 87, 98, 99, 100, 102, 103, 105, 109, 111, 113, 115, 125, 130, 151, 152

alone 6, 22, 54, 63, 78, 80, 84, 85, 91, 92, 101, 111, 114, 124, 131, 151

ancestors 70, 72, 131

ancestry 133

angels 77, 78, 84, 85

anger 5, 24, 27, 35, 48, 69, 73, 103, 111, 115, 116, 124, 125, 132, 140, 141, 144, 145, 152

antidepressants 13

apologize 26, 74, 130

argue 22, 56, 71, 73, 127

argument 105, 143, 148

arguments 25, 55, 101, 123, 127, 143

attitude 130, 151

authentic 5, 27, 102, 114, 115, 116

authenticity 103, 115

awakening 63

awakenings 10

battle 6, 13, 38, 77, 78, 79, 128, 129, 142

battleground 115, 119

battles 13, 78, 82, 128

beatitude 58

behavior 9, 16, 20, 23, 30, 34, 35, 69, 73, 83, 96, 102, 104, 113, 122, 123, 130, 137, 139, 140, 144

behavioral 69

behaviors 6, 9, 34, 64, 73, 83, 84, 122, 135, 155

bible 54, 70, 71, 77, 79, 87, 89, 91, 97, 98, 102, 135, 137, 139, 149

blessed 21, 47, 93, 113, 119

blessing 61, 62, 63, 64, 67, 142

blessings 14, 45, 92, 93, 126

boundaries 73, 74

brain 23, 58, 78, 79, 80, 95

challenged 105

challenges 47, 56, 105, 114, 137

challenging 95, 105, 114
child 15, 21, 37, 38, 39, 40, 46, 54, 69, 73, 74, 83, 88, 92, 98, 129, 130, 132
childhood 9, 38
Christ 47, 64, 66, 67, 74, 79, 81, 87, 90, 92, 94, 95, 97, 127, 130, 138, 139
church 9, 14, 15, 21, 23, 62, 68, 79, 82, 83, 96, 98, 99, 100, 101, 102, 104, 105, 151
churches 14, 17, 100, 102, 104
codependent 33, 48, 62, 126
colostrum 67
colostrum-like 67
comforts 20, 39, 41, 42, 153
commit 54, 64, 70
commitment 10, 46, 64, 65, 97, 144
commitments 15, 31
committed 6, 81, 103
communicate 24, 25, 26, 29, 34, 35, 51, 52, 53, 54, 56, 103, 106, 123, 130, 135, 143, 154
communication 24, 25, 26, 35, 42, 51, 53, 54, 55, 56, 57, 74, 143, 144
communications 26, 35, 52, 53, 55, 56, 58, 59, 73
compassion 113
compassionate 144, 146
condemn 63, 139, 140
condemnation 5
condemned 16
confess 55, 154
confesses 90
confession 55, 103, 133
confidence 10, 45, 54, 74, 91, 100
confident 38, 87
confrontation 31, 72, 112, 149
confrontations 125
conscience 39, 45, 89, 106, 117, 130
consciousness 10, 20, 38, 40, 84, 111, 117
consequences 21, 72, 78, 121, 139
control 15, 19, 20, 21, 22, 23, 24, 29, 32, 33, 35, 38, 45, 48, 49, 51, 53, 56, 62, 63, 64, 65, 66, 70, 78, 79, 94, 95, 122, 127, 131, 146

counselor 82, 111
counselors 123
creator 42, 74, 89, 94, 147
crisis 33, 109, 110, 122, 124, 126
deliverance 61, 62, 63, 64
delusion 9, 46, 48, 78, 120
denial 31, 32, 33, 71, 82, 105
depressed 29
depression 13, 29, 33, 48, 141
descendants 72
detox 116
detoxification 100, 116
discourage 25
discouraged 25, 95, 151
discouragement 114
discussion 15, 17, 37, 57, 61, 106, 120, 121
discussions 5, 63, 80, 83, 102
disobedience 38, 56
doctor 30, 67, 111, 122
doctors 29, 30
doctor's 100
drama 34, 35, 83, 124
dramatic 64, 114
drug 5, 15, 16, 24, 89
drugs 5, 13, 15, 16, 21, 24, 42, 73, 74, 77, 79, 115
drunk 23, 30, 72, 77, 78, 89, 111, 121, 122, 124, 144
drunken 101, 121, 131
drunkenness 22, 23, 61
dysfunction 26
dysfunctional 147
Eden 37, 78
embarrassment 31, 102
embryo 40
embryonic 42
emotion 113
emotional 6, 16, 31, 39, 53, 57, 58, 62, 72, 73, 74, 101, 106, 113, 130
emotionally 6, 25, 29, 30, 33, 65, 73, 113, 124, 141
emotions 53, 61, 101, 120, 141, 147

empathetic 101, 105
encourage 15, 71
encouraged 17
encouragement 16, 87, 95, 110, 130, 137
encourages 72, 106
enemies 41, 128, 129, 153
enemy 54, 80, 91, 128, 129, 130, 134, 144
environment 6, 10, 15, 26, 33, 55, 57, 63, 69, 72, 73, 106, 119, 120, 146
environmental 69, 72
environments 101
evil 37, 39, 77, 79, 80, 81, 83, 84, 85, 89, 95, 109, 119, 128, 129, 130, 131, 141, 144, 153
expectation 48, 56, 57
expectations 5, 10, 48, 106, 114, 127, 135, 153
failure 6, 33, 45, 56, 91, 103, 130
failures 135
faith 13, 97, 98, 106, 107, 128, 132
family 5, 6, 7, 9, 10, 11, 13, 14, 15, 16, 17, 24, 25, 26, 27, 29, 30, 31, 32, 33, 34, 35, 39, 40, 42, 46, 52, 53, 56, 58, 62, 63, 64, 65, 69, 70, 71, 73, 74, 77, 78, 79, 80, 81, 82, 83, 85, 87, 89, 94, 95, 96, 97, 98, 99, 100, 101, 102, 103, 104, 105, 106, 109, 110, 111, 114, 115, 116, 117, 119, 120, 121, 122, 123, 124, 125, 126, 127, 129, 130, 132, 135, 140, 141, 142, 145, 146, 149, 151, 155
father 37, 38, 40, 42, 47, 69, 70, 81, 87, 88, 90, 93, 94, 95, 98, 107, 117, 127, 129, 138, 139
fear 30, 31, 41, 65, 82, 85, 105, 114, 117, 127, 135, 141
feeling 16, 22, 23, 24, 35, 38, 43, 46, 52, 53, 70, 73, 91, 119, 125, 128, 143
feelings 6, 11, 14, 20, 25, 32, 34, 35, 36, 38, 40, 41, 45, 46, 47, 48, 49, 53, 57, 72, 73, 77, 88, 91, 92, 100, 101, 102, 103, 104, 105, 106, 114, 115, 125, 129, 139, 153
fellowship 66, 130, 134, 155
financial 31, 72, 100, 121, 123
flesh 19, 20, 38, 40, 42, 45, 48, 51, 73, 80, 88, 90, 94, 119, 129, 151, 153
food 23, 42, 56, 73, 93, 94, 106, 131, 132, 145, 155
forgive 139, 140, 151, 152
forgiven 139, 140

forgiveness 26, 83, 139, 140
Freud 67
friend 25, 39, 54, 60, 93, 94, 96, 97, 110, 113, 115, 119
friends 15, 25, 32, 33, 47, 63, 70, 72, 73, 81, 97, 105, 114, 116, 122, 134, 138
friendships 21, 25
frustration 11, 13, 19, 24, 25, 26, 95, 100, 124, 144
generation 38, 69
generations 38, 142
genetic 16, 41, 42, 69, 70, 71, 72, 126
genetics 9, 69, 70
genome 70
God 5, 7, 9, 10, 11, 14, 16, 19, 21, 23, 24, 37, 38, 39, 40, 41, 42, 45, 46, 47, 48, 51, 53, 54, 55, 56, 57, 58, 61, 62, 63, 64, 65, 66, 67, 68, 70, 71, 74, 77, 78, 79, 80, 81, 83, 84, 85, 87, 88, 89, 90, 91, 92, 93, 94, 95, 98, 99, 102, 105, 106, 107, 109, 110, 112, 113, 114, 117, 119, 120, 121, 124, 126, 127, 128, 129, 131, 132, 133, 134, 135, 136, 137, 138, 139, 140, 141, 142, 144, 145, 146, 147, 148, 149, 151, 152, 153, 154, 155
guilt 5, 14, 37, 73
habit 81, 126
habits 20, 135
handicapped 31, 78, 133
heart 9, 14, 24, 26, 35, 39, 41, 42, 62, 63, 90, 91, 93, 111, 116, 117, 129, 139, 140, 142, 144, 146, 152, 153, 154
heaven 39, 40, 42, 66, 84, 88, 93, 95
heavenly 14, 42, 128
heavens 138
home 6, 13, 14, 15, 21, 26, 29, 30, 31, 34, 35, 48, 52, 56, 64, 67, 70, 82, 85, 93, 101, 102, 106, 110, 112, 115, 120, 122, 123, 124, 125, 127, 128, 131, 134, 138, 141, 144
hope 5, 10, 14, 20, 21, 24, 30, 31, 32, 33, 39, 42, 45, 46, 48, 55, 57, 66, 67, 81, 84, 94, 106, 114, 115, 116, 119, 125, 126, 130, 131
hopeless 5, 10, 11, 33, 67, 117
hopelessness 5, 11, 20, 117
humble 54, 58, 60, 66, 81, 84, 88, 96, 103, 109, 124, 151
humility 58, 60, 63, 65, 88, 95, 116
husband 48, 84, 87, 127
husband-wife 45, 56, 88

husbands 81, 131
indulgence 20, 23, 39, 62, 70
indulgences 62
inheritance 69, 70, 71, 126
inherited 16, 38, 63, 129
insanity 48, 121, 135
insurance 81, 105, 116, 121
intention 66, 116, 144
intentional 52, 58, 131, 142
intentionally 58
interdependence 133
intervention 17, 35, 81, 82, 93, 109, 110, 111, 112, 113, 114, 115, 116, 117, 121
interventions 109, 111, 112, 113, 114, 117
isolate 17
isolated 124
isolates 24, 78
isolation 14, 45, 72
Jesus 19, 24, 40, 51, 54, 64, 66, 79, 84, 87, 88, 90, 91, 93, 94, 97, 117, 127, 139, 141, 149
job 9, 14, 26, 31, 34, 42, 52, 72, 91, 93, 94, 100, 113, 122, 127, 130, 137, 138, 143
language 24, 51, 52
legacy 72
lord 57, 65, 66, 69, 85, 90, 91, 112, 126, 128, 131, 132, 139
love 5, 10, 11, 14, 16, 19, 23, 24, 25, 32, 33, 35, 45, 46, 47, 69, 72, 74, 81, 82, 85, 87, 90, 95, 97, 102, 106, 114, 115, 117, 129, 130, 147, 154
lovers 47
manipulate 37, 56
manipulating 106, 121
manipulation 29, 52, 114
manipulative 29, 41, 107, 143
marriage 5, 14, 15, 32, 42, 46, 47, 71, 82
marriages 71
meditate 58, 91, 92, 98, 154
meditation 90, 91, 92, 142
miscommunicate 52, 54
miscommunicates 34

miscommunicating 52
miscommunication 35, 52, 105
misperceptions 9, 11, 100
moderate-drinking 21
moderation 24, 63, 64, 71, 77
mother 9, 40, 41, 47, 51, 127
mouth-at-the-door 144
nagging 13, 78, 80, 122, 146
nonalcoholic 22, 24, 29, 48, 61, 103, 104, 126, 130, 131, 144
obsession 119
obsessions 95
overcome 13, 42, 84, 88, 139, 148
overcomers 14
parent 21, 33, 37, 38, 39, 54, 73, 74, 82, 83, 88, 103, 104, 132, 137
parents 15, 16, 37, 38, 52, 69, 72, 73, 74, 104, 106, 122, 127, 129,
    130, 137
passive-aggressive 112
pastor 30, 63, 82, 104
patience 6, 51, 53, 54
peace 5, 6, 11, 13, 14, 25, 34, 37, 38, 39, 40, 42, 43, 45, 51, 53, 56,
    57, 58, 59, 62, 66, 82, 83, 88, 90, 94, 107, 113, 125, 126, 127,
    128, 130, 131, 133, 145, 153
pharmaceuticals 13
pharmacy 77
pornography 81, 83, 153
powerless 34, 65, 78
pray 6, 10, 23, 54, 55, 57, 58, 73, 80, 81, 82, 84, 85, 87, 89, 90, 91,
    94, 98, 117, 120, 126, 128, 134, 140, 141, 146, 149, 151, 153, 154
prayers 14, 54, 84, 90, 92, 128
pre-alcoholic 72
pre-alcoholics 71, 72
pre-Christian 66
pre-Christians 67
pre-milk 67
professional 30, 100, 111, 112
professionals 100, 112, 114
rebellion 69, 95
rebellious 16
redemption 65, 73

relapse 11, 13, 14, 106, 119, 120, 122, 123
relapses 119
remorse 21, 30, 93, 109
repent 62, 65
repentance 63, 66, 83, 95
repentant 26, 30
repented 83, 93
repents 25
resentful 14, 25, 38, 102, 125
resentment 24, 93, 127, 140, 142, 152
resentments 103
respect 19, 73, 93, 131, 137
respectful 137
responsibility 61, 119, 122, 123
righteousness 90, 128
romance 5, 23, 24, 46, 47, 56, 83, 131, 153
romantic 46, 47, 83, 89
sacrifice 6, 46, 88, 117, 128, 129, 139
salvation 13, 14, 63, 65, 86, 95, 128
sanctity 125, 129, 131
sane 58, 65, 92, 99, 116, 125, 127
sanity 11, 21, 62, 63, 64, 97, 133
Satan 67, 80, 84, 88
secrecy 34, 73, 121
secret 84, 103
secrets 73, 106
secular 81, 102
self-image 73, 74
self-pity 96, 136
self-sufficiency 133
selfish 21, 32, 46, 47, 48, 51, 62, 71, 84, 93, 131, 153, 155
selfishness 88
serpent 6, 37, 38
serpents 53, 85
sex 19, 23, 25, 42, 46, 53, 87, 105, 155
sobriety 11, 13, 14, 15, 21, 25, 33, 34, 61, 62, 63, 64, 65, 66, 67, 68,
    79, 92, 93, 97, 100, 101, 102, 103, 105, 119, 120, 121, 122, 124
society 9, 39, 41, 68
sorcery 77

sovereign 74
sovereignty 137
sponsor 101, 105, 122
sponsors 105
spouse 14, 25, 31, 32, 33, 46, 74, 137
spouses 32, 33, 34, 137
stress 14, 72, 91, 113
stresser 22
stubborn 93
stubbornness 47
success 14, 22, 23, 26, 45, 62, 63, 68, 114, 115, 125
suicide 22, 48, 80, 81, 109, 152
supernatural 119
tantrums 145
teen 32
teenage 82
teenagers 32
teens 15, 32, 73
temptation 9, 19, 20, 30, 66, 71, 78, 98, 120, 139, 151
temptations 79, 129
tendencies 41
tendency 39, 69
therapist 9, 110, 111
therapists 17, 29, 30, 48, 100, 111, 121
tolerance 23, 146
transference 61
treatment 9, 29, 35, 48, 61, 62, 63, 100, 104, 110, 115, 116, 125
trust 57, 73, 85, 94, 98, 100, 132, 140
trustworthy 121
twin 58
twins 58, 69
ungrateful 68, 93, 146
unhappy 16, 111
unity 36, 37, 42, 46, 47, 87, 88, 89, 129
victim 109, 123, 130
victims 79
victory 6, 14, 56, 63, 66, 89, 113, 139
violence 81, 82, 83, 123
vulnerable 119

warning 32, 71, 113
warnings 21, 110
weakness 13, 133
weaknesses 5, 53, 55, 84, 129, 154
wife 9, 13, 47, 48, 52, 87, 127, 131
willingness 6, 33, 42
willpower 20, 21
wisdom 6, 10, 37, 38, 60, 134
worries 38, 91, 101
yada 87, 88

youth 16, 29, 95

43984213R00095

Made in the USA
San Bernardino, CA
04 January 2017